Two Women, Two Worlds

With hopes for one world of
understanding!
    Audrey McCollum
    October 23, 1999

Published by
Hillwinds Press
Etna, New Hampshire, 03750

Book design by Julia Hill Gignoux, Freedom Hill Design
Map and photographs by Robert McCollum

First edition: 1999
10 9 8 7 6 5 4 3 2 1

Publisher's Cataloguing-in-Publication Data
Provided by Quality Books, Inc.

McCollum, Audrey T.
Two women, two worlds: friendship swept by winds of change /
by Audrey McCollum; illustrator Robert McCollum.
—1st ed. p. cm.
Includes bibliographical references.
Preassigned LCCN: 98-93628
ISBN 0-9666896-0-7

1. Papua New Guinea—Social life and customs.
2. McCollum, Audrey T.—Journeys—Papua New Guinea.
3. Women—Papua New Guinea—Social conditions.
4. Kuru, Pirip.
5. Women's rights—Papua New Guinea.
I. Title.

DU740.4.M33 1998   995.'305
QBI98—1468

Two Women, Two Worlds

Friendship Swept by Winds of Change

AUDREY McCOLLUM

HILLWINDS PRESS

DEDICATION

For Bob, my beloved husband,
and Pirip, my dear friend.

ACKNOWLEDGMENTS

This book could not have come into being without my husband, Bob. During our travels, his interest in Papua New Guinea reinforced and complemented my own. His sincerity, kindness, and warmth helped us make meaningful connections with the people we encountered. His patience and persistence guided us through the frustrating glitches. And his skill at photography provided us with vivid images of our travels when we were home.

During the five-year evolution of the manuscript, he read and critiqued every chapter I wrote, and his affection, understanding, and optimism buoyed me through my gloomiest days. Other family members, too, and many friends have read portions or entire drafts of the manuscript and have offered the encouragement and constructive criticism I needed to persist. To these people I give heartfelt thanks: Karen Bernhaut, Cindy McCollum, Doug McCollum, and John Spellman; Nawrie Campbell, Steve Gordon, Marianne Hirsch, Jim Hornig, Norrie Kells-Gordon, Mary Kilty, Alex Levin, Elsa Luker, Lynn MacGillivray, Joan Snell, Virginia Swain, Susan Vogt, and Mariana Zantop.

I am also grateful to Timothy Bent, Phyllis Deutsch, Susan Leon and, most especially, to Susan Moore for editorial consultation.

Bob and Pam Bates, co-owners of Trans Niugini Tours, and their staff in Mt. Hagen patiently helped us work out our independent travels in Papua New Guinea. Some of their outstanding guides became friends, and have been mentioned in the narrative. We were received with warmth and generosity everywhere we ventured, but, unfortunately, many areas we explored could not be described in this story.

The anthropological studies that greatly enhanced my understanding of Papua New Guinea are cited in the bibliography with appreciation.

I am most grateful to the men and women who served as Pirip's scribes for fifteen years while we exchanged letters. The correspondence which has been included in the book has been lightly edited.

Finally, I thank Julia Hill Gignoux of Freedom Hill Design for her enthusiasm and creativity in steering me through the intricacies of design and production.

CONTENTS

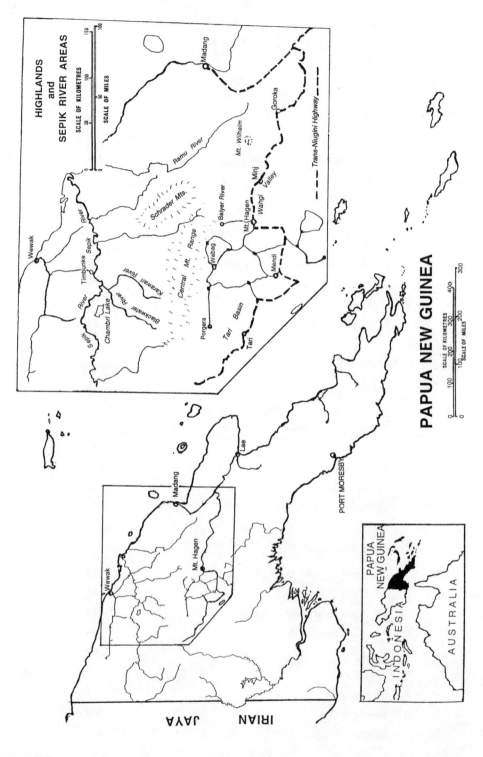

HIGHLANDS
and
SEPIK RIVER AREAS

SCALE OF KILOMETRES

SCALE OF MILES

Madang

Goroka

Mt. Wilhelm

Mini

Wahgi Valley

Mt. Hagen

Baiyer River

Schrader Mts.

Central Mt. Range

Mendi

Wabag

Ramu River

Sepik River

Timbunke

Wewak

Karawari River

Blackwater River

Chambri Lake

Porgera

Tari Basin

Tari

Trans-Niugini Highway

PAPUA NEW GUINEA

SCALE OF KILOMETRES

SCALE OF MILES

Madang

Lae

Wewak

Mt. Hagen

PORT MORESBY

IRIAN JAYA

PAPUA NEW GUINEA

INDONESIA

AUSTRALIA

REACHING

PROLOGUE

The equatorial sun is burning through the mists that swirl out of the surrounding forest. A shaft of light from the doorway of our thatch-roofed lodging dances across the highland woman's full lips as she speaks; it reflects off the dome of her forehead and the dark flesh cushioning her cheekbones. She leans forward, her voice low and intense.

"People ask, 'Why do this white woman and white man come to see you so many times? Why do they contribute to your center for women?' They say, 'Maybe they are your own father and mother come back from the dead.'" She pauses, studying my face.

"I understand those questions, Pirip," I answer. "When we traveled in Indonesia before we first came to Papua New Guinea, we went to a small island where they see few people from outside. Bob and I walked through a village, and afterward the headman went to our leader and said, 'This lady, she has white skin and white hair, so we think she has no blood. We think she is a spirit from the dead.'"

Pirip laughs, exposing both rows of startlingly perfect teeth, but her amusement has an uncertain edge. I wonder if she is more than a hair's breadth away from such beliefs herself. After more moments of silence, Pirip looks at me intently, her ebony eyes glistening.

"I wish," she says, "I wish that you really *are* my mother."

Hopefully my face conveys how touched I am, because words elude me. I'm shaken by the horrors my friend has described—cruelty and deadly violence. For hours, her disclosures have been blazing through the mists of uncertainty that swirled around our relationship for thirteen years. At last I understand her mission.

◈ ◈ ◈

I first met Pirip in a limbo of disconnection. Strange as it seems, our lives crossed because my husband, Bob, was urged to move from

3

Connecticut to New Hampshire and become dean of the Dartmouth Medical School.

For Bob, that was fresh opportunity at a time when he felt encroaching staleness in his professional life. Unlike many of his peers who made great leaps across the land to develop their careers, he had followed a steady trajectory from apprenticeship to leadership at the Yale School of Medicine in New Haven. But after twelve years as chairman of the Department of Epidemiology and Public Health—a position whose demands were as cumbersome as its title—it felt like time for change. He was mired in a dilemma about his next direction when he was asked to go north, and the challenge intrigued him.

The image of my future was hazy but I disregarded that. It was only 200 miles up the interstate, after all, not like moving to Kansas or Peru. When our son was a high school ski racer, we drove into those forested mountains 10,000 times, so it seemed, and exulted in their beauty.

Together we appraised our New Haven lives with a strangely cool detachment. The flaws, frustrations, actual dangers (I had been street-mugged twice within a year) came into sharp focus. And our offspring were fledging from the nest. It seemed the right time to go.

But still . . .

It was the leaving. The sun had begun shining on my life when I arrived in New Haven thirty-two years before. I came to start a job at the Yale Child Study Center and maybe, unknowingly, I was drawn by the city's name too—a new haven for a woman reared in a shattered family that had lurched from one crisis to the next.

Among three sisters, I was the impish one, the feisty one. I was the curious one, destined to become a psychotherapist. Longing to understand the melodrama my parents had played out in New York City, I also hoped to help others in ways I could never help them.

Life truly brightened when I married and reared our daughter and son. And the rhythms of my professional life were synchronized with my children's changing needs. There were many joys: after-school walks with our son to a woodland waterfall where he would confide the triumphs and disappointments of his days; sailing with friends on Long Island Sound and, when summer's torpor lightened the breeze, giving over the tiller to our daughter's eager hand; bittersweet tones of "A Bridge over Troubled Water" wafting through her bedroom window as I tended the scarlet blaze of tulips just outside.

The South African playwright, Athol Fugard, held us in thrall as he portrayed the tragedies of apartheid at the Yale Repertory Theater. And we visited street fests in the Italian quarter, savoring the oregano-drenched aromas from the pizzerias, and watching exuberant processions of people carrying statues of their saints on holy days. We joined carolers—black and white—at the New Haven green on Christmas Eve.

The strands of my life were woven into a richly textured fabric. A move would rip that apart.

Bob was a feminist before the word was bruited about. "If you don't want to go, I'll simply say no," he declared. "I *don't* want to go," I whispered while he slept. Dread was stirring, a legacy from my childhood. I didn't understand the dread, but I resisted its grip. "I don't want *not* to go," I said out loud, avoiding the choice he offered.

He accepted the job.

Wrenching loose began on that day—months of detaching from people and places that really mattered. Swamped with good-byes, we claimed a long-overdue vacation. Bob knew of a small ship, the M.S. *Lindblad Explorer,* that carried adventurers to mysterious places that couldn't otherwise be reached, so we embarked on a voyage through remote Indo-Pacific islands. It was the strangeness that lured us, as though we were making a bungee jump into our uncertain future.

The thrill of that leap pulled us back again after we moved to New Hampshire, and in Papua New Guinea, an island-nation north of Australia, I met Pirip Kuru. A feisty person she was, struggling to lead highland women away from the ancient rhythms of tribal life into a modern world of power-through-cash. Her quest was quite different from mine, but we were each turning away from the past and facing an uncertain future. We seemed to move toward each other, both reaching, both searching . . .

At first contact, Pirip crooned and patted my knee as our interpreter spoke: "Pirip says she never dreamed that an American woman would come here and talk with her." When I last saw her, Pirip planted a moist kiss on my cheek, saying in English, "You are like a mother to me." Those gestures, those words, bracketed years in which we connected, disconnected, reconnected. Separated by millennia of tradition, barely sharing a common language, we groped for understanding through our meetings and letters; we were often frustrated and frequently confused. And each time I felt I disappointed Pirip, specters from my past began stirring.

My urge to understand Pirip's strivings, and Bob's fascination with his own discoveries, fueled seven monthlong journeys to Papua New Guinea during those thirteen years. Dense rain forests and precipitous mountains have spawned countless distinct cultures and over 700 different languages in a nation the size of California, and we traveled far away from Pirip's home and her clan. We saw people existing in harmony with the natural world, living richly textured lives without manufactured goods. Yet wherever Bob and I ventured in this young nation, the clash between ancient and modern was the central drama, played out against a backdrop of sexual tensions— and Pirip was present in my thoughts.

At first, I supported her goal of bringing rural women into the spreading cash economy. Then doubts began to stir. Rapid Western-style development seemed to be stripping influence away from women and a sense of significance away from men. But when Pirip finally confided her private story, I saw why her struggle was needed. I also fathomed the central question for her, for me, for her country and mine; namely, how can the exhilarating possibilities of change be balanced with the sustenance of tradition?

And I discovered more. My new friends began asking, "Why do you keep going back to New Guinea?" The effort to understand my attachment to Pirip pulled me into a quaking bog of childhood memories, and then guided me onto firm ground again. In the end, that courageous mountain woman's affection lifted a timeworn veil of guilt and brought a calming self-acceptance.

Chapter One

PAYBACK

Our Twin Otter aircraft—feeling as fragile as the model planes our son glued together when he was seven—threaded its way through jungle-cloaked mountains at 8,000 feet. Tossed about by swirling updrafts, we stared uneasily at the precipitous ridges that loomed around and above us, almost grazing our wings. Then the summit of Mt. Wilhelm soared into the sky, piercing the roiling clouds at nearly 15,000 feet. It is the highest peak in Papua New Guinea and, close as we were to the equator, it seemed to be frosted with snow.

We made one landing between Madang, our port of entry on the northeastern coast, and Mt. Hagen, the principal town of Western Highlands Province. An arresting landing it was, on a grassy slope almost hidden among the surrounding peaks. As we dived down, a sudden squawk sent a tremor through most of the twenty bodies aboard.

"Don't worry," said Pip Smith—a friendly young Australian whose daredevil husband was about to fly his helicopter around the world—as she leaned toward me across the aisle. I must have been looking aghast as I reached to the seat behind me and groped for Bob's hand—warm, strong hand with broad fingers and raggedy nails. "It's only the stall warning," Pip said.

"*Only* the stall warning?"

"It really is all right," Pip said. "They have to cut the air speed quickly to get into an airstrip this small, so the stall alarm sounds." I tried to look reassured, but I doubt that I succeeded.

"You mustn't worry. We have two good Aussie pilots up front."

By now we were on the ground and my bladder was barely resisting the pressure of fear.

"Would there be a ladies' room?" I asked Pip, and she talked to one of the pilots strolling toward the shedlike terminal. There was a brief conversation inside, and I was handed a key that introduced me to the enchanting lingua franca of Papua New Guinea (PNG). It was Melanesian pidgin—*tok pisin*—an amalgam of Melanesian, English, and German words that reflects the country's history and also gets directly to the point. *Haus Pispis* was blazed into the wooden label attached to the key. Praise be, *haus pispis,* found just in time!

Airborne again, we were soon approaching the mile-high Wahgi Valley. Bracketed by the Kumpor mountains to the south and the Jimi range to the north, walled off by looming peaks to the east and west, it followed the Wahgi river for over sixty miles. This was the cradle of agriculture in the PNG highlands, where swampy river flats were yielding a surplus of taro, the earliest indigenous staple, more than 9,000 years ago.

◈ ◈ ◈

The first Caucasians didn't glide down from the sky. They stumbled in on foot. Although a succession of Europeans and Britons explored the coasts and major rivers of this daunting island from the sixteenth century on, questing for slaves, spices, and gold, deep penetration was impeded by the tangled terrain.

Nonetheless, the western half was annexed by Holland in 1828. Then in 1884, while tribal people were following their ancient rhythms of birthing, mating, and dying; of gathering food and building shelter; of organizing war and celebrating peace; of extending their trading routes; of harmonizing the material and spirit worlds, the eastern half of their island was summarily divided between German and British colonial rule. The northeastern sector became a German protectorate named New Guinea. The southeastern sector, called Papua, was claimed by the British.

Australia accepted administrative responsibility for Papua in 1904, and incorporated New Guinea, too, at the end of World War I. Some Australians yearned to harvest the protectorate's riches, but the land offered little welcome. From both north and south, swamps or densely forested lowlands rose toward a volcanic spine that was thought to be too wild to support human life.

So it was with astonishment that Mick and Danny Leahy, Australian prospectors avid for gold, discovered populated valleys hidden within the mountains in 1930. It was with astonishment that dark-skinned highland people confronted men so pale that they seemed like spirits of the dead. The highlanders' amazement was barely relieved when they realized that the wan creatures were probably human too. "Their skin might be different, but their shit smells bad like ours" were the graphic words translated by a witness.

Alien pale men, who had little in common with highlanders beyond elemental bodily functions, were to become a permanent presence here. When no accessible treasure lodes were found in the Goroka and Asaro valleys, the Leahy brothers took to the air in a Junkers plane and scouted farther west. After nosing their way anxiously through billowing clouds, much as we had done today, they had their first view of the verdant Wahgi Valley. Their appetite whetted by that sight, they returned on foot in 1933 with James Taylor, an officer of the Australian administration, leading a long line of indigenous carriers from the east. Half a century later, we scanned the same landscape with tingling anticipation.

◈　◈　◈

It was March in 1983. At the Connecticut home we'd left behind, lemon and mauve crocuses usually bloomed on St. Patrick's Day, and forsythia buds would be swelling. But in New Hampshire, where we now lived, there was no throb in March. Coming out of the deep retreat of winter, the light began to blaze. But spring didn't happen. They called it Mud Season instead.

Today, landing in Mt. Hagen near the head of the valley, we saw scarlet poinsettias taller than a standing man.

There was a glitch in our transportation so we were taken first to a hotel near the airport. It was a modest place with a commanding name, The Plumes and Arrows Inn. We were given tea and biscuits and, to help us pass the time, Peter Spencer, the Australian owner, started up a videocassette on his VCR. Mr. Spencer had prevailed on a Hagen clan to adopt him as a member, and, in the video, he was shown joining in a *singsing*, the celebration of a ceremonial exchange. His pale face was hidden behind scarlet, black, and white designs. With a mother-of-pearl crescent and strands of animal teeth around his neck, gaudy plumage soaring above the fur cap on his head, and a bone piercing his nasal septum, he was almost indistinguishable from the Hagen men as he stamped and chanted exuberantly to the incessant beat of their drums.

Two small blonde girls, perhaps two and four years old, ran into the lounge. They were restless and impatient, Mrs. Spencer told us, because they were not allowed to play outside.

"Are they being punished?" I asked.

"No, no, it's not that," she said, "although they may feel that way. It's for their own protection."

"From what?" I asked, and the story unfolded.

Not long before, there was a dispute between Mr. Spencer and a member of his staff, with anger on both sides. The national (the preferred term for native people) was fired from his job. Soon after, his own young daughter sickened and died.

"We didn't know what caused the illness," Mrs. Spencer said. "We supposed it was an infection." But the child's father thought along traditional lines; he thought of poisonings and malevolent ghosts. He thought of a person who might have paid a sorcerer, or made a sacrifice to a spirit of the dead, so that harmful powers would be turned against the little girl!. He suspected Peter Spencer.

"One day, the cook found an amputated finger in our refrigerator," Mrs. Spencer told us. I shuddered and she noticed.

"You see, it's the custom for highlanders, especially women, to chop off a joint of one of their fingers when there's a death in the family. It's meant to express their grief—but this was different."

"How so?" asked Bob. As a doctor, he was no stranger to mutilation, but he looked appalled.

"This finger was cut from the dead child's hand," Mrs. Spencer explained. According to the still-loyal members of her husband's staff, this was a sign of intended vengeance. One of the Spencer's own daughters would be taken in a *payback* unless the grieving father was compensated for his loss of a child.

We never learned the end of the grisly tale. But we heard about *payback* often as we traveled through the Wahgi Valley. Among the Hagen people who lived around Mt. Hagen, as well as the Kuma people who lived farther east around Minj, health, strength, fertility, and a large clan were valued above all else. Those qualities were fostered by an intricate web of social relationships that maintained credits and debts. It was believed that the well-being of clanspeople depended on maintaining a balance. Thus, gifts and assistance were always reciprocated. Injuries too.

◈　◈　◈

Our first local guide was Busy Bee, whose winsome name was conferred by a nun in the mission school he attended. Christian missionaries had followed the footsteps of Australian prospectors in the 1930s. But after outbreaks of violence between Westerners and indigenous people—each group mystified by the ideas and behavior of the other—the highlands were closed off for two decades until Australian patrol posts could be established. Only then did the missionaries bring in Western education, both secular and religious. But there were fees.

"My family was able to pay the school fees," Busy Bee said proudly. "I completed eight grades, and then I had one year more in a general vocational-technical program."

Busy Bee looked stolid, with a stocky, muscular body straining against his Western-style shirt and trousers, a broad nose, jutting brow, and the wide, wide mouth that seemed typical of highland men. He looked stolid, but he was bright, lively, and tended to be impish. English had become the official language of Papua New Guinea and his was fluent. He was eager to talk about his Hagen people and their customs.

We had ample time for talk, especially when he drove us fifty-five kilometers north from Mt. Hagen to the Baiyer River wildlife sanctuary. We jounced along a narrow, unpaved road in a Land

Rover, at times at the edge of a precipice. The Baiyer River gorge was hundreds of feet below, but I scarcely noticed the awful plunge in this exuberant countryside. Huge sunflowers bloomed on the banks, and tree branches were hidden by cascading golden blossoms. In the distance, mists boiled up and tumbled over the jagged mountain ranges—mists that presaged the afternoon rains.

Whenever we stopped to look, to feel, to record with our camera, people materialized from nowhere. They came running, smiling, wanting to shake our hands—there seemed to be dozens of eagerly reaching, clasping hands, and I liked the elemental skin-to-skin connection. Most wanted nothing from us but amiable contact.

But there was a shadow side too.

"If you hit a pig, the car will be noticed," Busy Bee warned us as we drove around a curve and almost grazed a trotting piglet. Most of the swine we passed were tethered by one leg. "To avoid *payback,* you must find the owner and give him compensation. A man without a pig is a nobody."

"If you hit a man, you must keep on driving or you will be killed in immediate *payback.*" He was oddly matter-of-fact. I would have guessed he was trying to titillate me except that I had heard the chilling admonition before. My shoulders and back began tensing each time we rounded a bend, and my legs ached to jam on the brakes.

Finally we reached the sanctuary. The entrance gate was ajar, and no guardian was in sight, so we roamed the 120 hectare (300 acre) rain forest preserve, pausing at fenced enclosures.

Amidst the tangled undergrowth we spied wild dogs like dingoes and various marsupials—reminders that New Guinea and Australia were joined by a land bridge until 8,000 to 9,000 years ago. One marsupial was a *cuscus,* a tree kangaroo. The size of a house cat, with amber fur, huge glittering black eyes, a pointed nose, dainty ears, and a long prehensile tail, it was a winsome creature.

Not so the cassowary, among the most primitive birds that live today. This flightless creature was one of the strange ratites, which include the emu, ostrich, kiwi, and rhea. It was an arresting sight, with a long blue neck rising from the coarse black feathers on its body, an orange wattle, and a bony crest rising from the base of its beak and extending high above its head. It was a fearful looking beast with large, curved claws. Stiletto-sharp, they could disembowel a man—and sometimes did, Busy Bee told us. It was an aggressive bird, too, easily provoked to attack. This one might be called the dwarf cassowary—*Casuarius bennetti* a small plaque informed us—but to us it looked huge. We didn't linger.

One enclosure was open, and a keeper was squatting on the ground near a coiled python. "Can I touch it?" I asked Busy Bee, and when he translated my request, the man smiled and beckoned.

"Why on earth d'you want to do that?" Bob asked, shrinking back as I moved toward the reptile. An unnerving encounter with a rattlesnake during his Texas boyhood had left a legacy of dread.

"I'm curious—I've never had a chance to touch a snake safely."

"How do you know this is safe?"

"I don't think the keeper will let it squeeze me to death, do you? He must know how to handle it." So I crouched down and ran my fingers along the creature's back—with the grain, so to speak, not wanting to ruffle its mood. "I've always thought snakes were cold and slimy," I told Bob. "It isn't. It's a little rough and kind of warm."

"It's poikilothermic," he said, looking slightly smug.

"It's *what?*"

"Poikilothermic." He was relishing the word. "It means the snake assumes the same body temperature as its surroundings." I felt like sticking out my tongue, but we were interrupted.

"Look over here," Busy Bee called out. He had wandered out of the enclosure and was pointing high into a soaring tree. Emerald, turquoise, and sapphire iridescence shimmered in the dappled light. "That is the superb bird of paradise—you are seeing the breast shield." We stood in silence. Among the forty-five known species of these aptly named birds, forty-one live only in New Guinea, and this was the first one we'd seen.

"Ohhh." Did that soft exhalation come from me or Bob? The look on his face was reverential, and I was feeling the same.

"Watch carefully," Busy Bee said quietly. "This is a display tree." We waited, but this jewel-like creature wasn't in the mood to flare his plumage and attract a mate. Then several different birds flew in, their tail feathers like fountains of rosy silk.

"Those are raggiana birds of paradise," Busy Bee said with a glitter in his eyes. Paradise plumes, plucked from male birds, were prized by highland men. They were presented at betrothals, marriages, childbirths, and deaths, or when new alliances were forged. The more valuables a man could present to others, the higher his prestige would rise, and the more securely his social bonds would be cemented. Paradise plumes had been so eagerly sought that the birds were now protected by national law. But the law was not enough. Sanctuaries like Baiyer River were needed too.

On the way south to Mt. Hagen, we stopped at a small roadside market. Women sat on the ground talking, laughing, tending their young, and bartering their produce: the staple *kaukau* (sweet potato), taro, sugar cane, bananas, and nuts from the betel palm— along with the powdered limestone and mustard leaves that activate the nut's euphoric effect. Two men who sauntered around seemed to have bleeding mouths; their saliva was scarlet and their teeth were stained red by betel chewing.

A young man with thick, curly black hair and skin like oiled walnut moved toward us, glowing with vitality. He was holding a bow and an arrow with three sharp prongs at its tip. Mindful of Busy Bee's warnings, Bob and I shrank back

"What are your weapons for?" Bob asked warily.

"It is for hunting."

"What do you hunt?" Bob asked.

"A person," the youth said with an up-curving grin. Busy Bee nodded.

"Tribal fights have broken out along this road," he told us. "But do not worry, they do not involve outsiders. Hundreds of people come to watch." Later in our travels, we'd be among such watchers.

Arrows used in warfare had single tips, Busy Bee explained. With its delicately carved three prongs, this man's arrow was likely to be used for hunting the birds, wallabies, and tree kangaroos that supplemented the vegetarian diet. But it could be used for *payback* too.

◈ ◈ ◈

The menace of *payback* grazed us closely after we moved thirty miles east in the Wahgi Valley to the town of Minj.

Peter Van Fleet, the manager, greeted us at the small Tribal Tops Inn, the only hostelry in Minj. After earning an M.A. in anthropology, he became an Australian patrol officer—a huge patrol officer whose height and girth would surely have been more intimidating than uniform or gun. When administration was given over to the newly independent nation of Papua New Guinea in 1975, his love for the country held him there.

"You're a medical doctor, I understand," Mr. Van Fleet said to Bob, who nodded. "Are you a specialist, then?"

"Well, my special interest is in infectious diseases like polio and hepatitis—especially prevention."

"Vaccines, you mean?" asked Peter (he suggested we call him that) and Bob nodded. "And you, Mrs. McCollum?" Peter's interest seemed sincere, so I explained my work as a psychotherapist, trying to help troubled people find satisfaction in their lives.

"We have two friends, both psychoanalysts, who worked in PNG," I continued. "They told us about the dramatic ways that boys were initiated into manhood. I'm fascinated by that and by the tensions they described between men and women."

"But let's start with people doing everyday things," Bob proposed in his "Down, girl" tone of voice.

Benjamin was designated as our guide around Minj, among the people known as Kuma. About five and a half feet tall, arrow-straight and full-bearded, he was a dignified man with a courtly manner. He was taught in the mission school how Westerners would expect him to behave, he told us in English that was precise and elegant in style. Benjamin was friendly too, and he seemed to appreciate our urge to see, hear, smell, taste, and understand as fully as travelers can. In the days to come he would take us among his *wantok,* the people who spoke a shared language, along with Paul, the driver. Still mindful of Mrs. Spencer's menacing tale, we were always glad for their presence.

We headed south one morning in air as fresh as the air around Denver or Mexico City was four decades ago—mountain air still unsullied by the yellow-gray miasma of "progress." Yet, I realized uncomfortably, the Land Rover supplied for our convenience might be emblematic of the future of Mt. Hagen and Minj. The national government, pressed by multinational business interests, was trying to catapult this young country into a cash economy and Western-style development—and we were helping that happen.

We headed for a settlement back in the hills. Most Kuma people preferred the ridges above the malarial river flats, and the accessibility of forests that yielded sticks for cooking fires and pandanus, or screw pine, for houses. Along the way, we passed a settlement near the dusty road. The Kuma didn't live in villages (although they were beginning to use that Western term). Rather, they lived in dwellings that might be far apart but were sometimes clustered together as these houses were.

Our eagerness had merged into impatience, so we asked Benjamin if we could visit here. After moments of hesitation—this hadn't been his plan—he told Paul to stop. That unexpected stop may have saved our lives.

Unlike the friendly highlanders who rushed toward us on the Baiyer River road, the few people who lingered around this settlement this morning seemed aloof, even suspicious, as we strolled around.

The most striking house was oval in shape, perhaps twenty-five feet long and up to fourteen or fifteen feet in width. Its walls were made of strips of pandanus bark, some blackened with charcoal and then woven in an intricate design of dark and light. The roof was well-tended thatch, made from the coarse sword grass—*kunai*—that was rampant in the valley

"Could we go inside?" I asked Benjamin and he consulted a nearby man who was watching us closely. We saw the man nod. "The owner is away," Benjamin explained, "but this is a member of his family and he says you may go inside."

The earthen floor was covered with clean wood chips, and it seemed boorish to be tramping around in dirty running shoes. But the thought came a bit late, so we inspected the dim interior. A fire was smoldering in the stone hearth at the center, and near the fire there were sleeping platforms covered with woven mats. Fires burned constantly in highland dwellings; the nights were cold.

Among the simple implements stowed on the supporting rafters, an axe caught our attention. Set into a shaft that was decorated with intricately woven fibers, its stone blade looked ancient. It was the Hagen axe that we'd seen pictured—a ceremonial axe unique to the Hagen region. It was one of the valuables presented in the bride-price we'd soon be hearing about.

When we came out from the house, a small throng had gathered around the Land Rover. An aura of tension enveloped us and we felt we'd done something wrong, but we didn't know how or why. It was clearly time to leave.

Not far up the road, another group had gathered and it blocked our movement ahead. The talk sounded urgent, so Benjamin and Paul stepped out to investigate. Voices were raised and men made agitated gestures while Paul looked very sober. When Benjamin came back, his ebony skin had a grayish tinge and his calm seemed forced, as though he were suppressing an inner turbulence.

"We cannot go any farther," he told us. "The road is blocked farther along."

"Blocked? By what?" Bob asked.

"Perhaps it is a mudslide from some heavy rains," Benjamin suggested. That was believable enough, although his tone was unconvincing. He was quiet as we drove back north, and it wasn't until day's end that the real story was told.

"When we made our first stop, one man went up the road to the village I intended to take you to. He told the people we were coming. Some news came back along the road—if we had gone to that village, we would have been stoned.

"*Stoned?* Just because we're foreigners?" I asked, appalled.

"It is more than that," Benjamin said. "Perhaps it is best that Peter Van Fleet should explain it to you." So after he and Peter had conferred, while we left rain gear in our cabin, we joined Peter in the lounge.

"What happened was this," he told us. "The people in the first settlement you stopped at recognized that the car came from Tribal Tops. Tribal Tops is owned by Peter Spencer in Mt. Hagen. The clanspeople of the man he fired, the man whose daughter died, live in the village you were going to visit. They were going to take revenge on Peter Spencer by stoning you. It's *payback*."

"Could we have been badly hurt?" Bob asked.

"Yes indeed," said Peter. "They might have stoned you to death."

I slept fitfully that night, forcing my thoughts toward the discoveries that lay ahead.

Chapter Two

BILUM/, BRIDE-PRICE, AND A WOMAN'/ DREAM

As each afternoon advanced in the Wahgi Valley, women trudged along the undulating roads, returning home from the forests, gardens, or markets. Suspended from the crowns of their heads, coarse fiber net bags, *bilums,* bulged with enormous loads. One might be stretched taut with produce and extend the full length of a woman's spine. A second might cradle a baby, and a bundle of firewood might crown the woman's head.

There was an uncanny rigidity to the women's carriage. Their range of vision and their movements were restricted by their burdens, sometimes heavier than one hundred pounds. They turned their heads slowly and stiffly as though their necks had rusted in the afternoon rains.

It was said that highland men didn't carry domestic loads for a reason that made sense in their traditional lives—they strode ahead of their women and children, carrying spears, bows and arrows, ever prepared for attack from a hostile clan. But what about now?

"Men have stronger bodies," I said to Busy Bee. "Why do the women carry such heavy loads?"

"It is right that they should," he quipped. "A bride is so expensive."

"They must feel so much pain in their necks," I said later to Benjamin.

"They are used to it," he said calmly. "They have done this since they were young girls." Little girls as young as three were given a tiny *bilum* and encouraged to carry one *kaukau*—a sweet potato—home from the gardens where they helped their mothers tend the crops. By seven or eight years, they might carry thirty pounds.

The *bilum,* made by forming intricate loops from one continuous strand of fiber, was considered a symbol of the womb—stretchy and enduring. When a Hagen girl was preparing for marriage, special *bilums* were made by her mother and aunts. The bride presented these net bags to her prospective husband's sisters to express her hope for friendly relationships. That may have happened among the Kuma too, since many customs were similar among Wahgi Valley people.

Yet if the *bilum* was an emblem of connection among women, it looked to me like an emblem of burdened lives. I wanted to hear Kuma women speak for themselves and Peter Van Fleet offered to help. "I know a teacher who speaks English well, and she's interested in women's affairs," he told me. "I'll see what I can arrange."

Although telephone and telex had come to some PNG towns, most communication took place as it always had, from person to person, on foot. When Bob and I came back from a day of exploration, Peter had sent a messenger to the school where Betty Kaman taught. In turn, Betty sent out messengers to the homesteads, the gardens, and roadside markets to search out Pirip Kuru, an advocate for local women. An evening meeting was arranged.

We gathered in the inn at dusk. Betty, who looked stately in a scoop-necked, ankle-length sheath that followed the lines of her slender body, motioned me toward a dim corner of the low-ceilinged lounge. She was drawing Pirip and me away from her own husband and mine. Pirip's husband hadn't come, although a daughter and small son had—they wandered around, trying out well-worn easy chairs. We could see animated men drinking beer in the public bar that was connected by a pass-through, but the lounge was empty except for us.

Pirip was just over five feet tall, full-figured, and clothed in a *meri* (woman's) blouse—a puff-sleeved loose smock—and a wrapped skirt that covered her calves. Her broad, fleshy nose, her cheekbones and high forehead seemed oddly freckled until I took a closer look and saw patterns of dark blue tattooing. Her wiry black hair was cropped short, and a furrow ran across the crown as though her head had been dented by years of bearing *bilums*.

Pirip seemed dignified but shy, reserved but alert, her dark eyes gleaming with interest. She knew too little English to trust her own words, although her face conveyed that she understood many of mine. But she shared with Betty a fluency in pidgin. Betty was the interpreter of the three-way dialogue in our secluded corner—a conversation she first claimed for herself. She told me her story in English as formal and measured as Benjamin's.

"My husband is a graduate of the University of Papua New Guinea," Betty volunteered with her head held high. "He is a successful coffee grower—coffee is the most important export crop in the highlands, you know." Indeed, Benjamin had shown us sacks of coffee beans at the roadsides, waiting to be picked up, weighed on a portable scale, and exchanged for cash.

"And you—I understand you're an experienced school teacher," I said, and she gave a regal nod.

"I also have four children of my own," she added.

"So who takes care of them while you teach?" I asked.

"My family." She raised her brows as though the question was odd. "I sent to Australia for nursing bottles so I could continue teaching while they were babies." Now I was surprised. Highland women typically breast-fed their young for three years or even longer unless a newborn had a stronger claim. Those were years of being carried in the mother's *bilum* until the small one's legs were strong enough to walk, years of being included in the rhythms of the mother's days. But Betty had separated parenting and employment as I, reluctantly, had also done.

"And have you been married a long time?" I wondered

"Yes, quite long—twelve years," she told me. "When I married, my family was presented with many pigs, bird of paradise plumes, and 6,000 kina. That was my bride-price." She seemed to sit higher in her chair.

"The kina, was that cash?" I asked. The shell of the gold-lipped pearl oyster, the kina was now also a minted currency worth slightly more than one US dollar.

"No, pearl shells." It took her husband's family years to gather that fortune, Betty explained (while her husband, Philip, was telling a similar story to my husband). Today she would cost three times as much, she said with a tinge of pride in her voice. Was "cost" Betty's word or mine—a reflection of hearing Busy Bee say, "a bride is so expensive"? Later, I wasn't sure. But Betty's view of herself seemed laced with ambiguities.

She had described herself as an activist for women so, presumably, her voice hadn't been silenced. Yet it did become muted in the presence of men. When we joined them at the dinner table across the lounge, the conversation faltered.

"We will talk later," Betty reassured me quietly, "when we are back in our private corner." That suited me well, because I was being challenged by a large portion of gristly beef, difficult to dissect under its blanket of thick brown gravy. One chunk stayed endlessly in my mouth. I chewed and chewed, afraid to swallow lest I choke. In the end, I had to eject the mangled morsel into my napkin and then furtively drop it on my plate—and I was so involved with that fractious beef that I never saw how Pirip dealt with hers.

"At times I would like to be free and independent," Betty confided when we withdrew from the men after our meal. "For me, that might be possible. You see, as a professional woman, I could earn a salary, and if I returned to my parents they would accept me back. But that is only because they own land and coffee, and they would be able to pay back my bride-price.

"It would be different for a woman like Pirip," Betty went on, gesturing toward her companion. "Her parents would have distributed her bride-price among the family so they would not be able to pay it back. They would probably beat her and force her to go back to her husband."

"Beat her!" I watched Pirip, but her face was inscrutable—a dozen years would pass before she would start confiding the stark realities of her marriage. Yet I sensed that this woman was entrapped, or had been entrapped in the past, and I wanted to draw her into our conversation somehow. She had been a silent witness, sitting forward in her chair, hands on her outspread knees, dark eyes continuously scanning Betty's face and mine except for darting glances toward her children.

"You both have beautiful dresses," I said. The *meri* blouse and skirt that Pirip was wearing were made from a vivid brown, black, white, and yellow cotton print—mine seemed drab in comparison. The corners of Pirip's full lips lifted in a tentative smile and she spoke to Betty.

"She sewed her dress herself," Betty translated. "You see, Pirip is a churchwoman; her pastor encouraged her to become skillful on a sewing machine." Then Pirip began to dream, Betty said. She dreamed that Wahgi Valley women could learn to make better clothes than the secondhand garments imported by the bale from Australia.

"What's the reason for the secondhand clothes?" I asked.

"The missionaries and government officials have been teaching the people to cover their bodies." Betty explained in a patient voice.

"Yes, of course. But what did you wear before?" I asked Pirip, and she spoke to Betty.

"Pirip says they wore tapa cloth from special tree bark. Women's cloth came from the same tree bark as men's, but it was made in a different way." There was a new sparkle in Pirip's eyes as she talked on. "For celebrations, her parents dressed her with feathers and furs that they collected from animals; they painted her face and decorated her in a beautiful traditional style—they were dressed half-naked!" Pirip erupted into laughter that shook her sturdy shoulders.

"I notice the blue marks on your face—we call that tattoo. Was that done in a special celebration when you became a woman?" I asked. Pirip shook her head.

"Just decoration," said Betty. "Pirip sees her new skill in sewing as a symbol of moving into modern times," she went on, veering away from tradition. "She thinks women can produce clothing this way to be sold in the markets so that they can earn some personal funds."

Pirip went from woman to woman, and two hundred responded to her idea, Betty explained. The South Wahgi Valley Women's Association was formed, and Pirip was named President.

"So you are an important woman," I said to Pirip, and her smile curved like a quarter moon and lighted her eyes again.

Each woman earned two kina by selling her surplus crops in the market and contributed the money to the association, Betty continued. Then the association bought sewing machines and fabrics with those funds.

Now Pirip leaned farther forward and spoke in an urgent tone.

"She longs for textiles from America, and wonders if you could send her some," Betty told me.

"Oh Lord," I thought. I hope I didn't say it. I tried to explain how difficult it would be to send fabrics, but I floundered, knowing that my words didn't have much meaning. Pirip had no way to appreciate the distance from New Hampshire to New Guinea, the cost of shipping, or the probable import taxes.

Yet Pirip's hope was easy to understand. When Westerners first struggled into the highlands, they encountered people who had not even developed the wheel. Their first sightings of that contrivance occurred in the 1930s when Australian gold prospectors flew their planes in. It is said that tribesmen crawled under those strange big birds to learn whether they were female or male—that, at least, could be understood.

Those planes, and others that followed in World War II, were laden with cargo, products of Western technology. For a people with no experience of industrial manufacturing, this influx of goods seemed magical. If so much came unbidden, why not more in response to ritual and desire? Why shouldn't Pirip imagine that I could supply endless bolts of cloth?

But I couldn't, and when Pirip realized I was saying that, her shoulders sagged and she looked down at the floor.

"Tell me more about what you hope to do," I urged her, disappointed to be disappointing her and quelling an impulse to put an arm around those drooping shoulders.

"Pirip wants to help women modernize all their domestic skills," Betty explained. "We used to have a welfare visitor who does not come any more. Welfare workers are based in the towns, and they are ignoring rural women."

"Any special reason?" I asked. Betty didn't know the reason, but she did know that women needed them to learn about modern child care, hygiene, and nutrition. Anemia was widespread among women, and both infant and maternal mortality were high.

"Too high," I said. "This is one of the few nations in the world in which men live longer than women. Is there medical care for women?"

There was a Minj Health Center, said Betty, but going there required a long walk for most people, or they had to find the fare for the PMV—a public motor vehicle, typically an open truck filled with standing passengers.

Bob and I had already visited the health center and the male health aide who ran it answered Bob's questions readily. Immunization against measles, polio, diphtheria, tetanus, and whooping cough were available, and he had BCG (a vaccine against tuberculosis), the aide explained. He could provide treatment for malaria, diarrhea, and respiratory infections too, and a vaccination was being developed against the deadly *pigbel*—a bacterial poisoning that afflicted highlanders, especially children, after feasts of pork.

The center had much to benefit women and children, but all those immunizations and treatments must be paid for in cash. In the room labeled Children's Clinic we saw no children, only a group of men playing cards.

I described that to Betty, and she shrugged. "Few women have cash."

"What do they do about family planning?" I asked her. That would be a female matter, she told me. Depo-provera injections were offered at intervals, as well as IUDs and tubal ligations. But women couldn't use those methods unless their husbands consented and supplied the cash.

"But weren't there traditional ways?" I asked, knowing from my reading that women avoided sex by going on family visits or withdrawing into menstrual seclusion; they used herbal contraceptives or abortifacients (men believed they used magic spells); and they refrained from intercourse during the long interludes of nursing babies. Betty looked uneasy, so I didn't press. "What about contraception for men?" I did ask.

"Men do not consent to vasectomy," Betty said flatly.

"So how is the association of women progressing?" I wanted to refocus on Pirip's dream. She had been sitting quietly, her face impassive. Now she frowned as she talked rapidly to Betty in a low, intense voice.

"Pirip says that among the original two hundred women, many were beaten or threatened with beatings by their husbands—they fear that an association may bring about unwelcome change in their lives," Betty told me soberly. "Maybe one hundred remain in the association now.

"But Pirip is a strong woman. *Strongpela meri,* we call it in pidgin. In the last election, she became a candidate from her district for the provincial government—we have both a national parliament and a government for each province, you see. She did well," Betty went on. "There were eighteen candidates, seventeen of them men, and she ranked sixth in the count of votes. She will try again."

"The only woman—that's *really* well done," I said to Pirip. Her gaze held mine and a warm current of appreciation seemed to flow between us until Betty interrupted the moment. Pirip was dreaming of a center for women, she explained. When a parcel of land for lease was advertised by the government, Pirip applied and it was awarded to her. Together, Betty and Pirip stirred the interest of politicians. The Minister of Commerce and the Minister of Women's Culture were from Wahgi valley, and through Betty and Pirip's persuasions and the ministers' influence in parliament, a grant of 27,000 kina (about $34,000 at that time) was made for the center. But the funds never reached the women.

"I only learned about it indirectly, through my husband," said Betty. "He hopes to be elected to the government himself. You see, the funds were embezzled by one of the ministers, and he used them for personal investment. I do not have much hope that the funds will be recovered." Betty looked grim and Pirip was frowning again. "The Minister is involved in a court action, but he can afford the best legal representation."

"We have corruption in my country too, and it's most unfair," I sympathized. "So what have you done about the center?"

"We had plans for the center drawn up by an architect," Betty said. But, with the prices of building materials soaring, Betty and Pirip estimated that their building would cost at least 14,000 kina (or $17,500). "We sent the plan to a women's association in India. We hoped that they might support us, but there has not been any response."

Pirip was watching me closely, maybe reading the dismay on my face—these women could have no idea of the plight of Indian women. Then she leaned toward me and spoke urgently.

"Pirip asks, 'Is it possible that any help could come from America?'" She doesn't miss a beat, I thought, amused and admiring. And I was captured by the thought that women in the Upper Valley where Bob and I now lived—a region in New Hampshire and Vermont that straddles the Connecticut River—might reach 10,000 miles across the world and clasp hands with women of the Wahgi Valley. So I promised to take back the story of the South Wahgi Valley Women's Association and see if a small amount of financial help could be possible. While I spoke, Pirip moved very close; gazing directly into my eyes, she began crooning and caressing my knee. Then she spoke.

"Pirip says she never dreamed that a woman from America might come to Minj and talk to her," Betty told me.

Pirip studied my face intently. What did she see? A pale-skinned woman from across the world who was reaching for connection too?

◈ ◈ ◈

The wrench of our move in the States—the aching, longing lostness—had taken me by surprise. Separation from special people caused the deepest ache. My children were off at universities; they would have gone anyway. But I had left supportive colleagues who understood the challenges in our work. I had left clients who allowed me into the most private realms of their minds. I had left friends who shared the sadness and gladness of everyday life. Many among all those special people felt that I was abandoning them and, in truth, I was.

To gain perspective on my turmoil, I began interviewing other women who were relocating. I heard about joyful anticipation, but I also heard about sorrow, loneliness, and shattered identities among women who had dismantled their lives to accompany their men. They described their sense of disconnection in powerful words. "I feel like a ghost." "It's as though I'm invisible in this town; nobody here really knows who I am." "Your old friends take you as you are, good or bad; with new people you keep having to prove yourself." "I miss my dear friends so very much."

Even women in sturdy marriages need close bonds with other women, I learned. Intimate friendships, based on trust and mutual concern, grow slowly and are not easily replaced. A mover may be cordially welcomed, as I was, but still feel adrift and lonely, yearning for something unnamed.

Chapter Three

DREADFUL DESIRE

"There's going to be a courting party this evening. If you'd like, I can arrange for you to attend," said Peter one morning.

"Please do!" I urged him. "Would Pirip have been involved in a courting party before she married?"

"Very likely," said Peter. So as daylight waned, the Land Rover nosed its way cautiously along narrow lanes to a small settlement where Peter led us into a traditional house—windowless, dark, stifling, and jammed with local onlookers.

"The ceremonies are called *tanim head* and *carry leg;* you'll see why," he said.

After we had found places among the throng sitting along the walls, five couples filed in. The crowd around us became denser as watchers jockeyed for good sight lines, and the only doorway was blocked by standing men. It seemed hard to breathe, my heart began pounding, and I felt a claustrophobic shudder deep inside. Fighting an impulse to bolt, I turned toward Bob for reassurance—he's usually a rock-steady sort of man—but he was staring rigidly ahead. He was thinking of fire, he told me later. A kerosene lamp was hanging on a pole; if it were jostled loose, there could be a conflagration.

Fortunately, the throb of an hourglass-shaped *kundu* drum diverted our attention. The couples knelt side by side, then sat back on their heels. Full-bearded men and boys faced one direction, girls the other, and now I saw how Pirip had once been decorated for ceremonies "in a beautiful traditional style—dressed half-naked."

Skirts composed of multiple strands of twined fiber fell gracefully between the girls' thighs, and amber *cucscus* pelts hung between their high, taut, pubescent breasts. They wore necklaces of animal teeth and earrings of fluffy white feathers. But like an emblem of the modern world snaking through the hills, bright red circlets adorned one girl's ears. They looked a lot like plastic.

The males had narrow fiber aprons called *laplaps* suspended from their intricately woven bark belts, and bunches of straplike tanket leaves stuck in behind. *As gras* was the apt name—it was more shameful for a man to expose the crack between his buttocks than to show his penis although, ironically, *as gras* drew the eye to the forbidden place like a magnet—the Western eye at least.

Youths of both sexes had painted red ochre masks around their gleaming eyes, and black cassowary feathers soared above their headbands of *cuscus* fur. One young man had even added the intact scarlet, emerald, and sapphire plumage of a lorikeet.

Among the watchers, a few men had seized the festive moment and decorated themselves too. Circular bailer shells adorned their foreheads, and kina shell crescents gleamed on their chests or at their loins. Boar's tusks hung at their throats, and one older man had thrust a semicircle of bone through his nasal septum.

Men secretly practiced love magic before courting parties, since they gained prestige if girls swayed toward them and invited them to *carry leg*. They lost face if that didn't happen. Sexual initiative belonged to the girls during this one interval in their lives, beginning with the first stirrings of puberty.

The young people began swaying toward each other and then away, toward and away, in response to the insistent drumbeat. Oiled brown bodies gleamed in the lantern's glow as each couple's heads turned in unison so that their noses met and parted. Then each girl rested her legs across her partner's right thigh, and they started *tanim head* once more. Over and over, again and again, the teasing motions spurred giggles and rising excitement. Other shoulders were swaying, mine included, and erotic energy pulsed through the crowd.

Pair by pair, the aroused couples would slip away to enjoy a night of passion. With one exception. The couple who giggled most intensely were only playing the role of a courting couple, Peter explained after we had quietly retreated to find some air. They were actually sister and brother. The sibling bond was intense—in fact, a

Kuma male saw himself as an incomplete human who was made whole through his connection with his sister's womb. But incest was *tambu*.

Marriage ended this idyll of erotic freedom for a young woman. Since the aim of marriage was to enlarge the clan, and since repeated inseminations by the same man were needed to spur his baby to grow in his wife's womb—so the Kuma believed—any risk of her adultery had to be avoided. A wife was even forbidden to talk with a man except in her husband's presence.

And sexual freedom wasn't the only thing lost in marriage. A girl's close ties to her mother—the mother whose sleeping compartment she may have shared until puberty approached—as well as her attachments to her grandmother, sisters, and brothers, were ruptured at the moment that she was led or forcibly carried away to her husband and his kin. If his homestead was several days' walk away, she would rarely visit her family again.

That image stirred a dormant ache inside of me, and I wondered about Pirip. Had she had lonely times too?

◈ ◈ ◈

"Benjamin would like to take you to visit a man named Patu," said Peter one day. "He's the father of Benjamin's second wife. Patu's wife died recently, and Benjamin has sent this wife to take care of her father. Everyone has an obligation to take care of his *wantok.*"

"Benjamin's second wife—is the first alive?" Bob asked.

"Oh yes, polygamy is still common in the Wahgi Valley," Peter said calmly. "It's a bit about prestige since it shows that a man is able to accumulate considerable bride wealth. It provides him with ties to other clans, too. And, well, you may know that it is *tambu* for a man to be intimate with his wife while she is feeding her baby, and that may last three years. So having more than one wife offers him outlets." And, I thought caustically, it provides agrarian workers and beasts of burden. I'd seen no four-legged beasts of burden, only women.

But now Benjamin had arrived. "Do your two wives get on well together?" I asked him as we jounced along a roller-coaster road—the Wahgi Valley was laced with ridges and vales.

"My wives get on well enough," Benjamin said.

"Are wives sometimes jealous of each other?" I persisted. "Busy Bee told us that his first two wives fought so much that he sent them both away and found a third. Of course, they are Hagen people."

"That can happen among my people too," Benjamin admitted. But his wives lived a long steep trudge from each other. Benjamin pointed out the separate ridges on which he had built a thatched hut for each wife—she shared it with her children and pigs, he said.

"Shares it with the *pigs?*" Bob couldn't contain himself.

"Yes. Each pig has a separate stall for the night," Benjamin explained. "They are house-trained so the stall stays clean."

"Fine," I said, "but the women live so far apart."

"That is true," he agreed, not catching my implication of loneliness.

We crested a final rise and the Land Rover bumped to a stop. There, in a strangely barren landscape—no trees, just a few charred shrubs—three buildings stood, starkly exposed. Benjamin led us toward Patu's house as people materialized from the surround.

Benjamin spoke politely to his wife but offered no hug, no affectionate smile. Yet when he turned to Patu, who had smeared his dark skin with gray mud to signify mourning, they clasped hands firmly.

To shelter from the fierce forenoon sun, we went into Patu's house—a windowless bush house with woven pandanus walls, a thatched roof, an earthen floor. The air was blue with smoke from the central fire. Eighteen of Patu's relatives crowded in behind us, most of them dressed in tattered Western clothing. One woman wore a loose bra outside of her T-shirt; another one's dress may have been a nightgown in Sydney, and probably arrived in the bales of cast-offs Betty had described.

We crouched in the gloom, joined in an awkward silence.

"Why did you come to my country?" a grizzled man asked. His forehead was heavily furrowed above large dark eyes and a thick nose with a bulbous tip. Nasal ornaments worn in a lifetime of ceremonials had pulled down his septum so that the nostrils flared out and upward; deep creases ran from their margins toward his chin like stern parentheses, getting lost in the fullness of his coarse, black beard. His torso was bare except for a kina shell crescent almost the width of his shoulders.

He asked the question in his *ples tok,* and Benjamin translated for us. Bob looked at me, his brows raised inquiringly. He's a pensive man, not always quick with words. I had no quick words myself just then, so I snatched at one of many truths.

"It is your custom to fight clan wars. In the whole world, men fight wars. We believe that if men and women can try to understand each other's needs and customs, maybe some day the wars will stop." Benjamin's translation produced a guttural response, "eh, eh," and nods that seemed to convey acceptance—by sheer luck, my answer connected with this family's recent experience. Benjamin told the story.

Patu had been a man of property, including a prized machine to extract coffee beans from the "cherries." He was developing a cash crop that would admit him to the modern world of *bisnis.* As his prosperity grew, *belihat*—anger, fire in the belly—was growing in a man of a hostile clan. We never learned the reason, but as his *belihat* smoldered, he gathered allies from within his clan, and then his fury ignited an attack. Before dawn, while everyone lay sleeping, Patu's homestead was ravaged. Unprepared to fend off the assault of barbed arrows and spears, he and his people fled. His land, crops, and dwellings were burned, his coffee processor destroyed, the coffee trees stripped of bark so they would die. Coming back to this devastation, Patu and his kin built new dwellings and planted new crops.

Now Patu broke urgently into Benjamin's tale. Since his wife was dead, he lamented, who would tend and harvest the crops, who would care for the children and pigs, who would prepare the food?

There were murmurs from the others, maybe sympathy for his plight. I couldn't wholeheartedly share it. "What about Nila's plight?" I wanted to ask, but Bob was the only man there who would surely have understood.

"How did Patu's wife happen to die?" Bob asked.

"She died of cancer of the womb," Benjamin explained gravely.

With great effort, he had persuaded Patu to take Nila to the distant Mt. Hagen hospital, a long, uncomfortable trip in a PMV. There her illness was identified. Patu didn't speak pidgin, and his *ples tok* wasn't understood. Confused, frightened, suspicious of Western medicine, and convinced that Nila's sickness was the work of malignant spirits, Patu took her back home. Nila soon died—in dreadful pain, I imagined.

"Please tell him we're very sorry," Bob asked Benjamin, and a tear coursed down Patu's dark cheek in response.

"She was given a Christian burial," Benjamin volunteered.

"And what does Patu believe about her spirit?" I asked.

"He thinks that her spirit stays nearby," Benjamin admitted with an edge of embarrassment. The traditional and persistent Kuma idea was that the ghosts of the dead lingered on, capable of malicious actions. Only after all their known relatives had died would the spirits be released, free to travel to distant mountains where their existence would be permanent and their intentions would become benign.

◈ ◈ ◈

"I will show you how my people make a garden," Benjamin announced one morning as we approached a hillside where people were at work. The men had already cleared this sloping plot of land by slashing down and burning off the vegetation, he explained. Steel axes, brought in by Westerners, had greatly eased those tasks. They'd broken up the heaviest clods of soil and dug interconnecting drainage ditches so that the hillside looked like a checkerboard.

"Do your people ever terrace their gardens?" I asked. "The hills are very steep." He shook his head, looking puzzled at the question.

"Sometimes the women tie themselves to a tree or a rock so they will not fall," he said.

"Tie themselves?" Bob looked incredulous, but Benjamin nodded calmly.

"And they dig pits in the ground and place their babies there inside their net bags," he added. He parked the Land Rover and we walked up, being greeted with friendly smiles.

Banana trees and sugar cane were growing at the edge of the garden; men planted and tended those crops, Benjamin said. As the "male" crops grew, men tied in the side shoots of cane, causing it to grow longer and stronger—two men gave us a demonstration. Then one of them scaled a notched pole to show how men encased developing bananas inside their own leaves, making the fruit grow larger and sweeter.

"Is it only by chance, in this land of male flamboyance, that two up-thrusting crops are considered male?" I put that question to Bob.

"Oh c'mon!" was his answer. He's less prone to flights of fancy than I. Yet crops low to the ground—*kaukau,* pumpkins, peanuts, and various greens—were planted, weeded, and harvested by women. Some women were planting *kaukau* now with simple wooden digging sticks. They were bending straight-legged from their hips or crouching down on all fours, and still managing to chat and smile.

"The men are just standing around," I said to Benjamin.

"You see, when there was a great deal of clan warfare, the men would stand guard while the women worked," he explained.

Now, I realized as we drove on, men hunted the occasional bird or marsupial with their bows and arrows; they built dwellings; and some worked for cash in the foreign-owned coffee or tea plantations that began spreading across the fertile valley after World War II. A few, like Betty's husband and Patu, had small plantations of their own. But we'd been seeing idle groups of men at the roadside, some crouched around a deck of cards throwing bets. And we'd been hearing about *rascols,* men without meaningful work who preyed on others, assaulting and stealing.

"It seems to me," I said to Benjamin, "that highland women work much harder than men."

"That is true," he conceded, "and it is only right. It costs so much to buy a woman." Those words were sounding like a Wahgi Valley mantra.

⬗ ⬗ ⬗

One afternoon, we lurched up a rutted mountain road to the settlement where Benjamin's parents lived—we would follow the same road with Pirip years later to plumb the mysteries of her life. After welcoming us with smiles and pats on our arms, his tiny withered mother fetched a key. The woven pandanus men's house was secured with a modern padlock.

We stooped low to enter, stepping over a high sill that forced a hostile intruder into a very vulnerable posture. An area in the back of the house, partitioned off and accessed by a hidden trapdoor, was a shelter for women, children, and pigs when the homestead was under siege by an enemy.

In the main space, the supporting posts and roof gleamed with black resins from the ever-glowing fires. Pigs' jaws, bronzed by the smoke, hung from the crossbeam. "This shows the number of pigs my father has given to others," Benjamin explained. There were three crude wooden beds and space for woven mats. This was where Benjamin's father and male kin spent daytime hours in sociability, and nights in sleep.

"Closer to town," Benjamin explained, "some men now sleep in family houses—the missionaries say they should. But many preserve the traditional way." Then he turned to Bob. "To sleep with a woman," he told Bob earnestly, "can cause a man to become weak."

⬗ ⬗ ⬗

Benjamin's solemn pronouncement expressed a dread of the sexual female that was widespread throughout the highlands—a dread that co-existed with desire.

Girls spontaneously and inevitably became women, highlanders believed. If I understood Pirip, there was no celebration at their puberty. But in boys, manhood had to be induced. Severing a boy's bond to his mother was the start.

Ties between Kuma boys and their mothers were close until

weaning. If the mother became pregnant again, the bond would be ruptured as the boy was swept off to his father's house—although indulgent fathers allowed frequent visits during the first year of separation. But if no more babies were born, a boy might sleep with his mother until his formal initiation into manhood. Philip, Betty's husband, had told Bob a little about the rites.

Incorporated into a major ceremony involving massive exchanges of pigs (it occurred about once a generation), initiations took place at variable ages. Boys might be young, or well along in their teens. When the time came, male relatives forced the initiates to circle a roaring fire in the ceremonial house; they circled closely so the heat and the smoke were intense. This was a "roasting" intended to cleanse the boys of maternal essence, even the fluids they had been exposed to in their mother's womb. Later, after creeping though a tunnel of trees that symbolized the birth canal, they were made to crouch in icy water and endure having their tongues scoured with stinging nettles. This ordeal, it was believed, rid them of the weakness caused by their mother's care.

"The rites of manhood are a lot more exotic than what goes on in the States," I said to Bob later. "But is the idea completely different? I mean, think of little guys starting day care or school—if they cry when their moms leave, other kids taunt them: 'cry baby,' 'wimp.' And older boys, what about the grueling training so many coaches put their male teams through?" We'd heard about that from our son.

"What about fraternity hazings?" Bob chimed in with the endearing eagerness that livens his voice and lights up his face when an idea captures him. He reminded me of a fraternity pledge in a northern university whose prospective "brothers" got him drunk, drove him far out into the countryside, stripped him naked, and left him in the snowy night with a dime taped to his leg to make a phone call when he roused from his stupor. He never did rouse.

Bob remembered medical reports of burns, heat exhaustion, alcohol poisoning, smothering, gunshot wounds—a ghastly array of illegal but persistent forms of hazing. We talked late into the night about the ways that boys are ushered into manhood in our own country, and the ways that maleness is reinforced, often by exclusion of women.

But why must masculinity be so staunchly defended? Why are women so dreaded? Those questions intrigue me as a psychotherapist helping both men and women untangle their lives, and they played across my mind after Bob had drifted off to sleep.

Kuma people believed that females were intensely sexual. Their attentions were desired—courting parties showed that—but their sexuality was imbued with danger too. Intercourse could age a man prematurely; it could cause his taut and shining skin—the hallmark of vitality—to crumple into flaccid folds.

In other ways too, the sexual woman was hazardous to men. Menstruating women had to withdraw into seclusion, protect men from their soiled skirts, and avoid walking through newly planted gardens. Among the neighboring Hagen people, the danger was even more acute. A women could use her menstrual powers for malignant purposes, men traditionally believed. She could sicken a man by deliberately tainting his food with menstrual blood (Bob looked a bit sick himself when I told him about that). Or, by having intercourse during her period, she could bring about his demise. Blood absorbed through his penis would slowly rise up in two columns that meet at his neck. These fragile columns could easily break, and then he would die.

So the women of Wahgi Valley had powers that men couldn't control. Might it be that Hagen and Kuma men had drawn the line against those dreaded yet needed powers by excluding women from their own flamboyant roles as ceremonial and political transactors?

Might there have been a pragmatic equilibrium between the sexes before Western winds of change began blustering through the highlands? Perhaps it was too late to know. The women of 1983 seemed enmeshed in social, economic, and political constraints as intricately woven as the *bilum*.

Women like Pirip—courageous, persistent, persuasive visionaries—were trying to struggle free.

Chapter Four

SEARCHING FOR CONNECTION

A traditional highland woman is in a sort of bondage," I told a semicircle of college students when Bob and I were back in New Hampshire. I tried to keep my voice level as I described the exchange of women across the world for shells, plumage, and pigs. I tried, but I could feel *belihat* leaking out like juice oozing through splits in an overripe tomato. Frowns gathered on the young foreheads, mostly belonging to women, and a hand shot up.

"You really mean women are traded for animals?" The questioner's face was pale. I nodded.

"It bothered me, too, when I heard it. But keep in mind how important pigs are—a man who doesn't own a pig is considered a nobody. And women rear them almost like children. In one remote place we saw a woman sitting on the ground with a bristly little piglet on her lap. She was bare-breasted, and the piglet raised its snout and began suckling."

"You have to be kidding!" Most of the class looked appalled.

"I'm not. And it looked natural, not grotesque. Women do that for a piglet that's puny or sick. Anyway, to go back to what I was saying, men earn prestige through lavish presentations of what's called bride-price—now it includes cash as well as pigs—so women get caught up in male ambitions. Then, after a woman is exchanged for her bride-price, she apparently becomes her husband's possession."

"Yet if women are exchanged for so much wealth, they must be highly valued in their culture, don't you think?" The quiet question came from Marianne Hirsch, a Dartmouth College professor who had invited me to talk with her Women's Studies class about women in Papua New Guinea.

Her idea was so startling that I gave a weak nod and let the question slide by. Then I told the class about a brave mountain woman named Pirip, struggling to free women from the tangle of tradition.

That evening, mulling over Marianne's question, I turned to *The Kuma* by Marie Reay, an Australian anthropologist whose own outrage seemed to ooze through her scholarly prose. Traditionally, Reay explained, the bride-price of a woman like Pirip would pass through several stages. Her betrothal, arranged between her family and the family of a man in a friendly clan, would be sealed by a presentation of plumes, kina shells, and pig meat from his family to hers. When the marriage payment was made by his kin, her family would make a reciprocal payment; then a woman from the husband's clan would be presented to Pirip's clan as a bride. When Pirip's capacity to enlarge her husband's clan was confirmed by the birth of her first child, his people would make a childbirth payment to hers. The reciprocal flow of valuables was complex and ongoing—*payback* in its positive expression, at least for men. The woman's part was immutable.

For her and others like her, only two routes of escape would have been possible. She could become a Wandering Woman, seen as a creature of insatiable sexual appetite who roamed the countryside trying to attach herself to a man. Or she could commit suicide, hurling herself into the Wahgi river. So if women were highly valued, as Marianne suggested, they were also tightly controlled.

◈　◈　◈

Marianne Hirsch had become a mentor during my first bewildering year in New Hampshire, showing me the scholarship alive behind the raucous football games, fraternity bashes, even some drunken rapes—celebrations of raw maleness in a college that had admitted women only a decade before. She and two colleagues, Brenda Silver and Mary Kelley, welcomed me into their classrooms to re-explore literature and history and discover unseen, unheard women of the Western world.

The Women's Movement had gained momentum in the 1960s, but I had scarcely noticed. Immersed in my New Haven life, I trod a balance beam between parenting and professional work when that was still uncommon. When my daughter was three months old and I returned to my office two mornings each week, I was looked on askance by psychoanalytic colleagues who doubted I was accepting my "feminine role." I didn't openly challenge their conviction that a full-time domestic life was ordained for women with families—I just kept showing up in my office.

Later, I was invited to present a paper at a national meeting of pediatricians, and it was well received. Afterward, though, a male colleague at Yale paused in the hallway to say, "I didn't go to hear you, I went bird-watching instead. But I understand you wore a very pretty dress." I didn't get mad for fifteen years.

My Dartmouth mentors showed me how often women's intellectual accomplishments had been veiled in the past, and that insight spurred me to get mad—finally—at my Yale colleague's deprecation. A "born-again feminist," I wryly labeled myself.

So I met Pirip with a heightened sensitivity to women's concerns; in turn, her dreams infused me with fresh purpose. While I'd been a withering transplant, she was yanking up her traditional roots and embedding herself in the modern, Westernized world. Her determination and energy were contagious.

In a letter, I told Pirip that I had written a story about her for our newspaper and had described her struggle to the Women's Network of the Upper Valley—an informal coalition of women who met monthly to support each other in their diverse aims. Many members made small contributions to Pirip's building fund.

I also encouraged her to consider a less costly center, perhaps one constructed in the traditional manner from pandanus and *kunai* grass, which could be interesting to travelers passing through Minj. Finally, I relayed questions from women who'd heard her story, and in two months the answers came.

17 July 1983

Dear Audrey,

Thanks ever so much for the unexpected letter. I really enjoyed our short meeting at Minj Hotel. I wished I could communicate with you in English so that I could ask questions about the outside world. Unfortunately I had to get Betty to translate my language to English. During our short time I wasn't able to communicate directly with you the points that I wanted to make because Betty jumped onto a different topic. Anyway, I am happy to correspond with you through letters. I got an aunt who is a senior school teacher who is willing to do the letter writing for me. . . .

Here are the answers to your questions.

My denomination of the church is Evangelical Brotherhood Church of New Guinea but I deal with women of all denominations. I regard them as one big group willing to work for the rights of women in PNG.

What do our husbands feel toward us?

It has been a custom passed from generation to generation that women were regarded by husbands as domestic care takers only and were not given a chance to take part in decision making. When PNG got Independence and formed her own government they passed a motion called the "Eight Point Plan" which says women in PNG will have equal rights as men. Educated husbands understand what it means to have equal rights but the non-educated husbands, it is hard to convince them. Through my women's group activities many husbands see that women are able to do worthwhile things other than caring for domestic affairs only.

My aim in standing as a candidate for Provincial Government was to fight for the "Rights of the Women" in my province. Many welfare officers and patrol officers saw me as a strong talker and a political minded woman. They advised me to stand as a candidate, so I did. Unfortunately I lost but I am not too upset. Being a village women's group leader I still fight to get women involved in group activities that can be done at a village level. I do not expect to get things done overnight.

My biggest problem is that I have no capital to start a bigger project I planned two years ago. We do not have a building of our own to come together and have activities. We have meetings under shady trees. I applied for land in Minj town and won a piece of land just beside the police station which is very safe. I've fenced it but the building for our center is not built yet. The plan that I sent to the Welfare Headquarters was just too much. Estimated cost of the building plus the activity sections was K50,000. The South Wahgi women's association cannot afford it so I am planning for a building which will cost K20,000 to start off.

At the moment some women are being ill-treated by their husbands—some of their little earnings are being used by husbands. My aim is to get women in groups so they do things with their own hands and sell them for money. When the income is in large amounts it can benefit every woman.

These are the programs I'll be carrying out when the center is built: sewing, cooking, making traditional artifacts, running a canteen as well as a milk bar. We will have regular meetings sharing ideas, finding ways of solving problems in our families and teaching our artifacts to young girls who come out of school and cannot get a job elsewhere.

There are said to be some women's groups in PNG but no group is advanced enough to give me a hand in financial aid.

I am not an English speaker and cannot read English therefore I have not heard of how women's groups in other countries are running their groups. I would be very much interested to hear and see films about women in the world and what they do.

This point is important. Betty is not in my women's group any more. She pulled out of my group as a vice-president. She is not co-operating with the women's group. She runs a business of her own and is also a school teacher. I am running the women's group by myself.

My letter is very long. I hope you won't feel tired of reading.

It may be best if you read it several times to understand my aunty's English.

I am looking forward to hearing from you.

With much love and wishes,
Pirip Kuru

Greetings from my husband and family. A special one from my secretary Esther Ambon (she's my aunt who will be writing letters to you from me)

I was awed by her ambition, and worried, too, because it seemed a set-up for disappointment. Yet it felt presumptuous to challenge her aims. Best, perhaps, to tell her more about women here.

I wrote back promptly, telling her that here, too, there are both men and women who would like married women to stay "as domestic caretakers only." Yet some women are doing work that was traditionally done by men—being doctors and lawyers, for example. Some husbands are encouraging; some are not, and then the marriage may end.

In the Women's Network, women describe their experiences in many different kinds of work, including domestic life. We explain what the problems are and where new opportunities can be found. We offer each other encouragement and concern.

Although we have advanced development, I wrote, women are not always treated as equals. Therefore, some members of the Women's Network contribute only to programs in the United States. But some think it would be wonderful to join hands with women in Minj, and I hope to raise about $400 for your association.

I then relayed more questions from women here, saying

I am asking you many questions, but it is from real interest and so that I can explain your needs to women here. I hope that you will feel that you can ask me any questions too.

You are a churchwoman. I am not one now, although in my childhood I went to church with my family. I don't really know what God is—perhaps God is everywhere in the world, in the mountains and trees and flowers and wind and rain and sunshine. I think Jesus was a remarkable man whose teachings about love were immensely important. But I feel troubled about things the church has done. In PNG, for example, the first missionaries tried to destroy many traditions and beliefs and spiritual objects, and I think that was wrong. I believe there can be many different ways of thinking about God and about life and death and spirits. Perhaps some day you will tell me about your own beliefs. Your pastor must be special to have such an interest in women. Here there are some women pastors now. Are there in PNG?

So from across the world I send my interest and concern about you and your kind aunt, and look forward to your next letter.

> With very warm greetings,
> Audrey

When I reread the letter, I wondered why I had described my religious ideas. Perhaps because I remembered Benjamin's embarrassment that Patu believed in spirits, as though he expected us to disapprove. Perhaps because I didn't know how solid Pirip's Christian beliefs really were and I had an urge to say, "We may not really be so different."

My own doubts about church ran deep. I dimly remembered Sunday school in the most fashionable Episcopalian church in New York City, and Easter services where, dressed in matching jonquil-yellow spring coats, my sisters and I mingled with the elegant worshippers of my parents' social circle. Fashion in churches, clothes, parties and travels defined their leisured lives: the "season" in Biarritz or St. Moritz where the international smart set gathered—children were sometimes included with the steamer trunks, watched by dutiful nannies; fox hunting in Virginia; glittering balls in Newport mansions. F. Scott Fitzgerald, my father's Princeton classmate, described it well.

On Sundays there was talk of brotherly love. But from Monday until Saturday, envy and malice often overcame compassion. Especially when the charade was ended by the Great Depression and the emptiness behind the frivolous lifestyle was exposed. When the gala parties ceased, the country houses were sold, the staffs of cooks, butlers, chambermaids, grooms for horses and nannies for children all dwindled away, church didn't help my brittle parents find new meaning in their lives.

In contrast, Pirip's church had started her in a fresh direction. But years would pass before she revealed the full shame-cloaked story.

◈   ◈   ◈

I feared that I'd overwhelmed Pirip with questions. The blaze of New Hampshire's autumn climaxed and faded, and we were in the icy clutch of winter before a letter came, with apologies for the delay.

Pirip's scribe, Aunt Esther, had been acting headmistress at her school while the headmaster studied at the university, the letter explained, and Pirip had been on the go. She had mustered a group of women to clean some government offices, but she was dissatisfied with the pay. So she flew to Port Moresby, the capital, to see some "very important people"—the Minister for Youth and Recreation and the president of the National Council of Women—about funds for her association. She stayed a month, but it was fruitless. She was told that the national government allocated funds only to the provincial government, and that did not recognize the South Wahgi Women's Association. It wanted headquarters established in Mt. Hagen. Pirip was undaunted. "I am still fighting for the right of the South Wahgi women to put up a center in Minj," she wrote. They had raised 1,200 kina so far.

> I asked the town planner if I could put up a bush material type house but he said no, because the land I got is in the centre of town and that house made of grass would spoil the good look of the town.

So when she had raised several thousand kina, she would start off with a simple, low cost permanent building. One room would be used to cook food for sale. In another room, artifacts from around PNG would be displayed. A third room would be a meeting place for girls and women to share their skills making string bags, weaving mats, and "modern crafts such as sewing, knitting, weaving and other skills that we don't know."

Now I would like to answer your questions.

We have a very good custom of caring for needy people like orphans, divorced wives etc. Any relation or a good friend can always give them clothing, shelter etc. The government does not meet their needs.

Some women in Wahgi fear the changes in the community so they don't respond to my group. Some women fear their husbands; if they join the group they will be beaten up or their bride-price won't be paid.

Most husbands control any income for the family, very few men trust their wives and give them money. When the women own some money they think of buying clothing and tinned food.

My husband is very encouraging and he's preparing to meet any changes in the future. By the way I got a small baby son. I got three sons and two daughters. My husband cares for them while I am busy with the women's affairs.

If I send you a cassette full of messages and music, would it be all right for you to play it and listen to it rather than writing pages of letters? You send the reply messages back to me in the cassette again, we'll be able to know more about each other at once.

So much for now. With much thoughts and wishes.

Yours faithfully,
Pirip Kuru—President, South Wahgi Women's Association

On sunny days, even in winter, I often sat on our terrace gazing at a smoke-blue range of mountains forty miles away. Crisply contoured, they reminded me of the peaks surrounding Wahgi Valley ten thousand miles away, and I sometimes imagined Pirip's figure taking shape among them. Her head, capped with dense, wiry black hair, supported the weight of a *bilum* bulging with produce, yet she walked resolutely. But after I read her letter, her *bilum* seemed to bulge with rocks—it dragged along the ground, heavy with obstacles opposing her aims: funds embezzled or denied, Betty's defection, threats from men that kept other women away. Yet Pirip's head supported that weight and, undaunted, she walked on.

Her strength was magnetic; it pulled me toward her. I wanted to draw it into my being; I wanted to understand its source.

I wrote to Esther to thank her for serving as scribe, and asking if she'd like to continue corresponding. I recognized my own ease in writing "pages of letters" on a machine, and paying for the paper and stamps, so I asked if she could find out what type of tape recorder was available in Mt. Hagen so that we could consider using cassettes. And I mentioned a possible return trip to PNG in the spring.

19 February 1984

Dear Audrey,

Thanks ever so much for your nice letter. It was a real surprise for me. In fact, I don't write to people outside my country because I don't have any friends to write to. I am very pleased indeed to communicate with you as a friend.

When I told Pirip that you are coming to PNG and even Wahgi Valley, I can't express how she acted. She couldn't believe me. I told her again and said, I am not lying. I am telling you the truth. Pirip was about to cry for joy as is our custom.

I personally feel that it would be very good that you come back to us. We really want you to come and live with us at home and meet the poor women who are trying to meet the changing world. There are so many things that we want to tell you but we can't write pages of letters. It takes time to write, but when you come you'll see things with your own eyes. I believe you'll have hundreds of answers to give to the women in USA after you visit.

I really would like you to coming during our first term school holidays so we would have time to visit the women together. My holiday is in April.

The house Pirip planned to build in town was rejected so we're still raising money to build a permanent house. Meanwhile Pirip's husband is building a traditional type house as you suggested.

Many women now realize that they need to change their present living condition. They would like to join Pirip's group but their husbands are not very pleased. Their husbands wouldn't allow their wives because they fear the changes in the culture and the religion.

I wish to hear more from you in the near future.

With much thoughts of you,
Esther Amban

I was dismayed. What had I said in my handwritten note that she took as a promise to return to Minj this year? Her idea of my staying with the women was on target, but it couldn't be done. I couldn't take my annual vacation in April because of professional meetings here.

Besides, Bob was eager to explore other parts of PNG. For him, our travels were both discovery and respite from complex pressures. Lolling on a beach wouldn't do it—unsolved problems might crowd his mind. A total time-out was what he needed, a fresh immersion. When they called from the college president's office and said, "Be sure and leave phone numbers where we can reach you," it gave him impish delight to say, "Where we're going, there may not *be* any phones."

So, reluctantly, I wrote Esther that we would have to come in late March. We would arrive by ship in Madang and sail on to the Trobriand Islands. Was there any possibility of a meeting in Madang?

I assured her of the continuing interest of the Women's Network, and expressed my hope of gathering more small donations for Pirip's center. She answered soon, but the mails were slow.

21 March 1984

Dear Audrey,

Hello and how are you? I am sure you are well. My dear I really want to meet you personally but I just can't due to other commitments. I've given permission to my husband Jonah Amban to come and meet you. He's dark skin and very big man. [Did she mean in stature or in status? Each sub-clan had a Big Man, who earned his position through skill at oratory and negotiation. He wasn't an hereditary chief but a consummate politician.]

Just to tell you a secret about the welfare leader who is with Pirip. She is . . . our big boss in the provincial level of women's affairs. But she never likes to share the national grant equally among our district groups. If you like to converse do so to Jonah and Pirip. Jonah can speak English so he may translate.

I am getting ready to go to Mt. Hagen for an in-service for senior teachers and head masters so I am not able to come with Pirip. I must attend this course as it is the only time allocated by headquarters. . . .

Pirip is bringing the bank pass book with her. You may either give cash or write a check into the account. Thank you very much indeed for your assistance. Again I ask you to use Jonah to translate to Pirip. He is a fair man. Won't mind at all.

I'll write to you later about why I don't want you to use someone else to translate.

With much thoughts of you,
Esther Amban

This conspiratorial letter hadn't yet reached me when we left on our next trip to PNG and I had little hope of seeing Pirip.

Chapter Five

PIRIP PERSISTS

There are visitors waiting to see you, Mrs. McCollum—they are outside of the security gate." This unexpected news reached me soon after our ship, the *Lindblad Explorer* again, docked in Madang. Bob and I walked along the concrete wharf and found a small group waiting outside the chain-link fence—two men, a young woman, and Pirip with a small nude boy suckling at her breast. I was stunned.

"Pirip, what a surprise; I didn't expect to see you." She beamed and clasped my arm.

One of the men stepped forward and, in fluent English, introduced himself as Jonah Amban, Esther's husband. Heavyset, he wore a blue knitted shirt pulled taut by his broad chest and muscular arms. He was clean-shaven except for long sideburns that curved below his red baseball-style cap.

"Pirip is deeply affected by the interest and support of a group of American women," Jonah explained as tears coursed across Pirip's smiling cheeks; they looked plumper than before. "This is Pirip's husband, Kuru," Jonah went on, gesturing toward the tall, lean, bearded man. The woman, whose close-cropped hair and maroon and yellow rugby shirt made her look boyish, was Pirip's nineteen-year-old daughter, Ruth—her firstborn child. Pirip's nursing son was a little over two.

"How did you get here?" Bob asked.

"Pirip is a strong talker," said Jonah, explaining that she had persuaded an official to loan her a government vehicle for this trip. "We drove for nineteen hours from Minj to Madang."

"Did you stop overnight?" Bob wondered.

"No, we drove straight through," Jonah said matter-of-factly, and it didn't sink in until later how grueling the family's trip must have been on rough highland roads.

"Have you had food today?" Bob asked. No, they had not. So we took them aboard the ship, into the dining salon, and asked for lunch for us all. When the food was served, a look of uncertainty crossed Pirip's face and was mirrored on Ruth's. Their glances darted toward the cutlery laid out on the crisp white tablecloth, so I made my motions slow and deliberate and the women imitated well. Except for meat. Pirip couldn't get the hang of cutting it in small pieces, so I did that as though she were my daughter.

After the meal, we moved out to the deck and sat under the shade of a canopy. The toddler explored the ship under the watchful but tolerant eyes of his sister, his father, and Bob, and then fell asleep in a deck chair; his guardians looked drowsy too.

Meanwhile, Jonah was interpreting for Pirip and me. Eagerly, she pulled a bankbook out of a small *bilum*—worn over her shoulder in the male style now—and showed me the Women's Association accounts.

"The members earned 700 kina cleaning up the jail and other public properties in Minj," Jonah explained. "Pirip has been assured that with your additional contribution of over 500 kina [the amount I wrote that I hoped to raise], the provincial government will provide matching funds."

"But I don't have the money with me," I said, dismayed. "I didn't get a letter before we left so I didn't expect to see you. It seemed safest to have the money transferred from the Women's Network account to your bank after we made contact again." Pirip sagged with disappointment, and I was appalled. Hope had fueled her long, exhausting drive, and I had let her down badly.

"Pirip has not wavered from her goal of building a women's center," said Jonah, his rich voice breaking a heavy silence. "With the help of the men in her family, she has already built a bush house center near her family house, and women have begun gathering there to produce artifacts for sale."

"That's good news," I told Pirip, longing to bring back her smile. "Some travelers would be interested in seeing how traditional artifacts are made; they might like to visit your center." Jonah translated, and then Pirip raised her head and spoke, but her voice sounded flat.

"Pirip wants to tell you that when she has accumulated the several thousand kina she needs, she will have a permanent building built on her leased land next to the police station. Then she will begin to develop the programs of education and mutual encouragement the women want."

Oh Pirip, I thought silently, so many women I know would have been crushed by the disappointment I've subjected you to—disappointment and maybe loss of face with the provincial authorities. But here you are, full of dignity, telling me you're carrying on. You're a stronger woman than I. But I didn't have the words to say all that in pidgin.

"Pirip, you're a *strongpela meri tru.*" I said that out loud and then she smiled. I was eager to understand what it was that sparked Pirip's vision of change in women's lives, but I couldn't frame the question in a way that made sense to her; she looked puzzled before she spoke briefly to Jonah.

"Pirip lived with a missionary when she was a child, and she went to primary school for two years," Jonah said; she nodded, but didn't add more.

"When were you born?" I asked after a pause, realizing I knew nothing about her early life.

"She does not know—there were no records then," said Jonah in a patient tone. "Maybe it was in 1947 or 1948."

"Were you born in Minj?" I asked, and then Pirip's voice seemed to flow through Jonah as he translated her words.

"I was born at Kamang Pingil River. The place is far—about fifteen kilometers from the nearest station, called Minj Station."

"Was that an Australian patrol station?" I asked. Pirip nodded again and went on.

"In the residential area where I was born we lived primitively."

"Primitively? Did Pirip use that word?" I asked Jonah.

"Yes. I am telling you her own words," he said.

"What do you mean by primitively, Pirip?" I persisted; that

word is so often used demeaningly. Frowning, she paused for a few moments.

"Men usually lived in the men's house—it included young boys too," she explained. "My mother and I lived far away from the men's house because the men had their restricting laws against women. My mother cooked food in pits—steam cooking."

"The earth oven called *mumu?*" I asked, and she agreed.

"Some of Benjamin's people prepared a *mumu* for us in the hills above Minj," I said, remembering the day vividly. Sticks had been shaved into a pile of tinder, then the Big Man of the group looped a strip of bamboo around a bundle of twigs. Grasping the bundle firmly with his toes, he pulled the strip back and forth, back and forth, until sparks flashed out and the tinder began to smolder. Soon a fire was blazing, heating large stones.

When the stones were glowing, women arranged them in a pit, using tongs made from digging sticks split at one end. They layered the stones with moist banana leaves, folding in corn, pumpkin, *kaukau, pitpit* (a wild cane that tasted like asparagus), and various greens. The feast was served on banana leaves. I described the scene briefly to Pirip.

"It was the same," she said. "My mother cooked *kaukau* and taro, greens we call *aibika* and others. We ate animal meat from the forest—*cuscus*, cassowary, some types of snake, fish from forest water, big birds."

"Your mother and you—were there other children in your family?"

"Yes. My father, Mr. Till Kingmind, was married to three wives but one of them died."

"From what cause?" I asked.

"Died in childbirth." Her tone was matter-of-fact.

"I'm sorry to hear that—was that your mother?"

"No. I was the daughter of the third wife, Mrs. Dakin. She gave birth to a daughter, which was me, and a son. That was my brother, Mr. Mike Till, who was the last in the family." Jonah wrote down the names at my request. "I had seven other brothers." Now, perhaps buoyed by my interest, Pirip leaned back in her deck chair and let memories stream out.

"In my life as a child I was told by my parents to look after the pigs; we had many pigs and they never stayed inside the fencing. Sometimes they went out destroying our neighbor's garden and the neighbors demanded compensation from us. So my daily work was to look after pigs."

Pirip and one brother, her father's first wife's second son, looked after the pigs belonging to all three wives, she said. Their gardens were in the "big bush"— the forest, far away from the place where they lived. "My parents told me that their work was to make new gardens and look after older ones. My work was to look after the pigs, and to break firewood and fetch water."

"How did you break the firewood—an axe?" No, Pirip explained, she gathered fallen tree branches, made them into a bundle, and carried them on her head. She fetched water for cooking and drinking from far away, collecting it in a length of bamboo. All those responsibilities held her back from going to the meeting places and the market—until the missionaries came.

"How old were you then?" I was still locked into our Western need for chronology. Pirip and Jonah conferred.

"Maybe seven years old. A year later my parents decided to put me in mission school. But my father was worried about me. Sometimes he stopped me from going to school because he thought the white-skinned people might take his daughter away. Later he realized that they came to be missionaries here and would not go back, so he let me go on schooling."

"So your father cared for you well."

"He did. My father treated me as a valuable wealth in the family; anything he owned was all mine. Sometimes he thought that I was the only one in the family." The memory had brought a glow to her face, and she paused for a moment, as though to relish it. "Yes, Father loved me very much, so sometimes he cut ripe sugar cane or banana and asked me to come in the *haus man* and sit down and eat with him—sometimes I sleep with him in the *haus.*"

"Even at night?"

"Yes, sometimes in the night. My father's love and concern was on me so much that he did not have concern about the seven brothers of mine."

"What work did your brothers do for the family?" I wondered.

"They would get slingshots and go out shooting bats and wild pigs and *cuscus*. They never listened to their parents, they went to find girlfriends."

"So your father loved you more, but he made you work harder than your brothers?" Pirip smiled but didn't answer. Questions about the shaping of her feminism crowded my mind but it was futile to push. Pirip and I were separated not only by language but by thought as well—different ways of finding meaning in our lives. And our interpreter was a man; maybe that constrained her.

Bob had led the others on a tour of the ship's bridge, and now they came back, eager to move on. So I asked Jonah to tell Pirip how much I admired her persistence and courage in working for women, and hoped she would tell me more of her story another time. When we began our good-byes, I sensed my growing affection for this woman from another world.

But I had let her down, and for me that's the stuff of nightmares.

◈ ◈ ◈

My father had been cursed by inherited wealth. When his fortune shrank in the 1929 stock market crash, he couldn't manage a transition from playboy to salaried worker. One night I saw him teeter on the windowsill, bellowing in a whiskey-rasped voice, "Look out below, here I come," while Mother clutched his ankle. Then he left and came back, left and came back, then left again—I never knew when it would happen or why.

The rent was paid, though our apartments grew smaller each time we moved to yet another fashionable address. And someone paid the wages of our last loyal servant, Harry Briscoe.

His skin was the color of bittersweet chocolate, his hair was grizzled. He moved as though his body ached, but he was as kind with children as with horses—he'd been our groom—and he learned to cook and clean and love us. I loved him back, yet I was often cranky when he woke us in the morning, and his eyes would fill with tears—he didn't deserve my meanness or understand it. Nor did I. And then he was sent away too.

Like many children of turmoil, I sometimes imagined that it was all my fault and it was up to me to fix it, whatever "it" might be.

My sister, Jackie, woke up sick when she was ten and a half. When I told our mother about Jackie's fiery spotted skin, she began phoning to find a doctor. We had no regular doctor and, in fact, no regular phone. In her slow slide into madness after our father left for the final time, Mother reclined all day on the living room sofa garbed in a rosy rayon negligee—lost in a reverie that gradually became demonic. She feared opening her mail, so the bills piled up unpaid. Utilities in our Park Avenue apartment were often cut off (Tennessee Williams would have loved the scene).

Waiting for the doctor, I dressed carefully in a clean blue pinafore—it had been my uniform as a summer-time city hospital aide. I filled a small glass with rubbing alcohol, covered it with a Kleenex, and plunged our thermometer into the sterile bath. It looked quite professional, I thought.

Jackie had German measles, the doctor said. After listening briefly to Mother's torrent of agitation, he turned to me. I was four-teen, after all. He glanced at my thermometer, although he didn't use it, and quietly told me what could be done to soothe Jackie while rubella ran its course. "She shouldn't read much," he cautioned. Her eyes were inflamed.

"But my homework!" she moaned. Our school had high stan-dards.

"Don't worry," I said. "I'll bring your assignments home, I'll read to you, I'll help you keep up."

But I usually lingered at school—it was a better home than home—and then there was supper to fix. Mother hadn't been reared to cook, and our older sister was away at college. When we were short of groceries because the Gristede's bill was unpaid, well, the corner delicatessen made up a fine muenster on rye.

The night before she went back to school, Jackie impaled me with her gaze. It was clear blue again.

"You promised to help me with homework every night. You didn't do it."

That wasn't the only time I failed to deliver some help I had promised. The promises were well-meant and she trusted them; but then, absorbed in my own concerns, I would disappoint her. And when she died an unnaturally early death, I wondered if my neglect had played a part.

◈ ◈ ◈

Now, years later, did Jackie's shadow lie across my relationship with Pirip? Pirip's eyes weren't blue; they were the color of strong coffee—between black and brown—with a lacework of pink veins through the sclera. Those eyes had searched my face during our first meeting in Minj. Then, when I spoke of a linkage between the Upper Valley and Wahgi Valley women's groups, her gaze became warm and trusting.

Had I really failed Pirip as grievously as it now seemed? Or had her disappointment pulled me into the swamp of self-reproach connected with long-ago failures? I wasn't sure of the answer, but the day after Bob and I got back to New Hampshire, I arranged for the $600 contributed by the Women's Network to be transferred to Pirip's account in Mt. Hagen.

I wrote her that the transfer had been made, but there was no answer. Four months later, I wrote again to Pirip and also to Esther Amban, asking if the funds had been received—I needed reassurance that this promise had been fulfilled. I also mentioned that women here might make further contributions. Two answers came.

Esther's letter protested that she had written twice and the letters must have been lost. But she could recall these important points:

> Pirip expressed her sincere thanks for the contribution from the Women's Network to the South Waghi Women's Association.

Pirip went through a big operation on her womb and stayed in hospital for one month. . . . she still felt weak.

Five members of the association resigned and got their money out of the association fund. . . . Their husbands didn't want them to stay in the group.

Pirip was renting a trade store to start making more money. She was using the women's association name but few were giving her a hand to get the business going smoothly. Pirip was trying her best with a few women and her husband.

Pirip found a piece of land to build a tourist centre. The houses were not built yet but the land was cleared. It was not in town but near the highway.

Esther concluded, once again in a conspiratorial tone,

Please don't refund the women's contribution which you mentioned . . . I've a different plan from Pirip's. I will let you know in my next letter when I've thought twice about it."

Then came this wrenching epistle.

8 September 1984

Dear Collum,
Hello and how are you. I am Ruth, Pirip's first daughter. Do you still remember me? . . .

Mummy is saying that she did say thanks a lot for the big amount of money you gave her. She told Esther Amban to write to you . . .

When we came up from Madang she got a very big sick and was in the hospital for two weeks . . . Doctor told her to go home again . . . after two weeks she went back to the hospital and stayed there two more weeks and they operate on her. They operate on her about three times. . . . When she came back from the hospital she quickly go and ask Esther, did you write any letter and Esther said yes. . . . But now Mummy finds that it is not true. . . .

When she received your last letter she was very sad and she cry. She is saying, if I were an educated woman I wouldn't waste time when I got your letter but I am not an educated woman and don't know how to write letter, so that's why I told Esther to write a letter and she didn't.

The very big point is that you don't get a wrong idea. The big money you gave, Mummy is putting in a club of her own with 15 members. The money is working at the store. The government said that any man or woman who apply for government ground can't do only little work. They have to start a big thing like a big store or super market. Mummy asked to do small things before but they said no, they said if you want to do it we get the ground back.

Esther came and asked Mummy to give that K500. She wants to buy a car or truck. For that reason, Esther is getting cross with Mummy. Mummy always thinks she wants educated women like Esther to write, but now I am writing. All of our family are sending greetings to you two. So Bye bye, God bless you.

I ached deeply reading that. My dear Pirip, I thought, I really have added to your burden. Maybe the grueling trip to Madang (made at my heedless suggestion) aggravated your uterine problem. Then I wrote to you in English when you're unable to write back yourself, and the slow postal service added frustration.

Now your government thwarts your efforts, and the Minj women don't cooperate—at least those things aren't my doing. Gritty woman, do you ever feel that there's more than you know how to manage? For me, that's a deeply familiar plight.

◈ ◈ ◈

One long-ago afternoon, when I sauntered toward our apartment building after school, I saw my mother standing on the sidewalk, sketchily dressed and trembling. Her face was contorted with fear. Nearby, the brown-uniformed doorman watched, his eyes brimming with pity. When his gaze caught mine, he shook his head slowly and gave a defeated shrug.

They were beaming rays through her body from Mars, Mother told me, desperate as a wild creature in a leg-hold trap. "Let's go back inside," I said, and she offered no resistance when I took one arm and the doorman the other, and we led her through the door, up the elevator, into our apartment—no real shelter for her since the rays might penetrate the walls. No use explaining that her eerie sensations were probably hot flashes from menopause, misinterpreted by her disordered mind. I'm not sure I'd even thought of that yet.

There was no one to help. Mother had no family and our father had vanished from our lives. Our older sister was in college, and it never crossed my mind to appeal to a teacher—too shameful to have a crazy mom. There was no family doctor and besides, Mother's psychosis was so insidious that she could persuade almost anyone that she was a rational woman—when she chose.

I was usually confused myself. Beams from Mars aside, what was reality in the threatening world she told me about, what was imagination? Bewildered, I tried to mother my mother; I tried to mother my younger sister. I didn't do either well. There were moments when resentment, even hate, spewed out, and guilt was the aftermath.

Guilt, and the hope of helping others in ways I could never help my shattered family. An expiation, perhaps, and sometimes it felt hard.

◈ ◈ ◈

It felt hard to help Pirip, but I wanted to persist. I wrote her in 1985, telling her that the Women's Network had contributed an additional $500, and those funds had been transferred to her account.

There was no answer, but I was deeply immersed in work—leadership in the Women's Network, writing a book about the impact of relocation on women, reading anthropology and the new psychology of women, and conducting a lively therapy practice. My friendship with Pirip had sparked fresh interest in each of those realms.

Then a letter arrived in 1986, seeming to speak in two voices. First was the voice of Betty Kaime, "a relative of Pirip Kuru and more like a daughter to her." She worked with the Provincial Women's Council, she explained, and was also secretary of the district association, where she helped Pirip with paperwork.

She and Pirip had inquired at the bank in Mt. Hagen, but the money I had written about had not been transferred to Pirip's account. The tellers told the women to write to me.

The association had bought a building, formerly the police beer club, from the Minj police department, and had applied to the provincial government for funds for renovation and developing a tourist center. They would start with three bush buildings and one permanent building, and they hoped I could help them contact tourist groups who would stay at the center.

> You have mentioned you wanted to return to Wahgi Valley one day. You can stay at our centre if we are ready. We are thinking about asking you to attend our opening at the center.
>
> Audrey, you may not believe it but we took a trip to Australia and have visited two states, Queensland and New South Wales. There were forty of us who went to Australia for the first women's group trip. We travel on a special discount rate return ticket.
>
> Find enclosed photos that were taken when in Australia and a copy of list of our registered women groups of south waghi district women associations.
>
> [Pirip's voice] I wish to apologize for not writing to you for a very long time. Betty, my daughter, who wrote to you before had some domestic problems to settle with her husband for the rest of last year, and the beginning of this year she was in one of our big hospitals. Had problems with her womb after giving birth to a baby dead some weeks in the womb and affected the womb badly. Now she feels well again so we are writing this letter in reply to your letter dated 15 July 1985.
>
> We are looking forward to hearing from you soon.
>
> Cheers,
> Pirip and Betty

Pirip's words hit home. Between my own two healthy children I, too, carried a dead baby in my womb. Late in my eighth month of pregnancy, the baby's movements stopped. No more flutters or glurps or throbs. No more guessing which tiny limb was thrusting against its confinement. Just a strange bulging stillness. Then a fetal electrocardiogram, the needle tracing a line as flat as the floor. An X-ray to confirm. I didn't see it; my husband did and came slowly to my bedside, his face glossed with tears.

"It's best to wait for spontaneous labor," the obstetrician said. I waited for a month.

Without sophisticated instruments to plumb her private spaces, did Betty sense that her baby was dead? Did she eat and sleep and work each day, moving, seeing, smelling, hearing, talking—an animate woman whose body was swollen with a tiny corpse? A corpse that was decomposing—so said my obstetrician, trying to reassure me that labor would be easy. I wanted to shriek, "Take that back! Take that back!" the way children do.

Fragments of death enclosed within life. A grotesque paradox.

I wish I had known that was happening to Betty; I would have written to offer sympathy. Hopefully, her kinsfolk had crooned some comfort. My friends could find no words; my colleagues asked, "How are you?" each day in the office, but they looked as though they hoped I wouldn't tell them and I rarely did.

◈ ◈ ◈

The money for Pirip seemed ill-fated. My bank could offer no explanation nor any way to trace the funds. Frustrated and sad, I wrote to Pirip explaining that the missing funds must have gone into some person's private pocket.

And, exasperated that I would disappoint her yet again, I explained that most American travelers make their arrangements in this country, and that it would be difficult for her at this stage to make agreements with foreign travel agents. Once more, I encouraged her to consider modest goals for now. Then I waited and wondered through another long silence.

29 September 1988

Dear Ms McCollum,

Thank you for such a nice letter. I am sorry that it has taken me a long time to reply to your letter of 9 November 1986.

We are very sorry that the money you sent to us has gone into the hands of some dishonest person as you were informed.

Betty divorced her former husband and got married to another businessman but this time she married a husband who had another first wife with many kids and has had problems since then.

I have won back my Wahgi Women's President position as I have done for the last fifteen years. Yesterday 29/9/88 at 2.30 p.m.

The Tourist Center you discussed with me is being worked on right now. One house is completed with three bedrooms and another two are still under construction. I am collecting hand-crafts and live wild animals, e.g. wild parrots, emu, possum etc.

Fencing is still to go and other items like bedding, small genera-tor and eating utensils. Next to our Centre will be our Handicapped Childrens Centre and the centre to assist the disabled children and old people.

You ask about how our women now earn money. Most of us haven't been educated to a stage where we can read and write English. But we grow cash crops at home, we raise poultry and pigs and pick coffee beans which is PNGs major cash crop. Wahgi sub province is the major supplier of coffee for PNG.

Women do what they like with their money, e.g. buy clothes etc.

Much of the money is spent on compensation payment. We have a custom of contribution by the whole clan or community. Also for bride-price payment which is well over K10,000 to K20,000. Then for the welfare of youth groups and women's association.

Men don't often interfere into women's affairs according to our traditional customs but always tend to help, e.g. my brother and my husband have given up work time to help build the centre for tourists for me. We don't have qualified carpenters but tourists will like typical Wahgi huts. Traditions of Wahgi Valley vary from the rest of the world.

Report of the money received:

I have received your first check of $600-K500 and have used it to buy a snooker table which costed me K1200. I spent my own kina to make up for the total cost of the table. It will be at the centre for tourist's recreation.

I am sorry once more the money got lost.

Last important thing: This letter is converted into English by Pirip's son in law. Hope you can trust him. A member of the Royal PNG Constabulary (policeman).

Will be hearing from you soon.

Sincerely,
Pirip

My heart sank at the news of the snooker (billiards) table. What a waste of hard-earned women's money that seemed; scarcely a visible center where women could meet, encourage each other, and learn new skills together. "C'mon Pirip," I wanted to write, "how will a snooker table help you? Was that your choice or the men's?" By then I understood that Kuma women traditionally allied themselves with male aims, furthering or impeding them as they chose.

It wasn't my place to tell Pirip how to use our help. But those grand dreams of a tourist hostel—had I unwittingly set those in motion because we used words in different ways? Or was that the result of government pressure to "start a big thing," as Ruth had written?

When I thought of Pirip, I often remembered her eyes. They were always on the move—scanning, searching, darting, sometimes wary, sometimes joyous. I wanted to try to see through those eyes, to see her world as she saw it. I wanted to see her center. And both Bob and I wanted more travel in her country. We wondered whether winds of change were blowing as fiercely in other regions, and how people were weathering those storms. We might, in fact, discover some interesting things to tell Pirip.

I wrote her that we would return to PNG in March, 1989, and would like to visit her. No letter came back, so we started out with guarded hopes.

DOUBTING

Chapter Six

HAUS WIN

W e drove eastward out of the tumult of Mt. Hagen, where our
plane had landed. There was a hubbub of traffic this year—
cars and PMVs and grinding, belching trucks that spewed black
diesel vapors into the morning freshness.

New roadside businesses had sprouted at the outskirts: tires and
batteries for sale, and shops for automotive repair. And in the
bustling market the few elderly men who sported *as gras* wore it
protruding below a western-style shirt or jacket—an entrancing
sight.

Finally we were speeding along the two-lane Highland Highway,
past silver-pink plumes of *pitpit* swaying at the roadside. To the
north, the intense but monotonous green of tea plantations was
more extensive now, as well as broad swaths of coffee trees. But to
the south, a patchwork of forest and agricultural plots still climbed
into the mountains. We saw sweeps of the coarse sword grass, or
kunai, that moves in when forest is cleared, and fountains of delicate bamboo arching up from the grasses. In the distance, clouds
swirled among the jagged pinnacles of the Kumpor range, with limestone gleaming through the jungle-clad slopes.

Turning south off the highway, Agua, our driver, stopped at the
Minj market to ask where Pirip could be found. Then, as we moved
slowly down a side road searching, there she was. When I called her
name from the Land Rover, she stopped, her mouth gaped in disbe-
lief, and then she began to cry. As I flung open the door and leaned
out toward her, she hugged me tightly, her shoulders heaving with
sobs. Her tears trickled down my neck, flowed inside my tank top,
and oozed into my bra—an oddly intimate communion. I hugged
her back and haltingly produced a pidgin greeting.

"Mi anamas tru long lookim yu gen" (I'm very glad to see you

69

again). She stopped crying momentarily, stared in open-mouthed surprise, and then wailed and sobbed more intensely than before, clinging to my arm.

"This is our customary way to show when we are happy to meet," Agua explained in a kindly voice. Then Pirip began walking beside the slow-moving Land Rover and guided Agua to the dirt lane that entered her family compound. He eased the vehicle along the track and parked near a traditional building.

The newly built women's center was in a clearing beyond. *Haus win,* meaning rest house, Pirip proudly called it in pidgin. It was a handsome heptagonal structure. The outside walls, made of strips of pandanus woven in an intricate pattern, were joined by vertical beams. Glass windows had been set into two of the walls. The peaked thatched roof made of *kunai* was topped by an upthrusting ornament—a style I had seen on men's houses and had taken to be a phallic symbol. Pirip's male kin had built this house.

People were crowding through its single door and appearing from under the surrounding trees with Kuru, Pirip's husband, in the lead. The center of his ebony beard was frosted now and an ultramarine blue knitted cap was pulled down to his ears. He bounded forward laughing and shouting and hugged me, holding my cheek against his until my face was wet from his tears.

Next Kuru's mother, a tiny, frail woman missing several teeth, moved close and grasped my hands. Studying my face, she began an eerie keening: "eh, eh, eh, eeeee" on a rising tone, held at the highest pitch. That was another expression of pleasure, said Agua while I enjoyed the exuberant welcome from these warm, expressive people.

I slipped a gift over Pirip's head—a black, scarlet, and gold bead necklace that reflected the colors we saw most often in highland bodily decoration. Then, with Pirip eagerly nudging my arm, we gathered inside the *haus win*—Kuru, his brother Gabriel, Pirip's son-in-law Chris, Bob, and over twenty women.

Most of the women wore *meri* blouses and skirts, but two were adorned for festivity. With their headdresses of lorikeet and paradise plumage and their blazing scarlet noses, it looked as though two birds had flown into a trade store and dipped their beaks in acrylic paint. But the illusion stopped at the neck; skirts of twined fibers hung gracefully from bark belts around the young women's hips, and fur pelts were suspended across their breasts. I guessed that Pirip had arranged this to show me how her parents had once decorated her in a "beautiful traditional style—dressed half-naked," as she told me at our first meeting, and I caught her eye and smiled. I would have winked, but that might have had meanings I didn't know.

Simple wooden chairs were brought in for Bob and me, while the others either stood or sat on woven mats covering the earthen floor. I felt foolishly enthroned—like a Queen Mum pretender—but resisted an urge to join others on the floor, unsure how that would be interpreted.

Everyone looked at us expectantly, so Bob expressed our delight at being there. Then he gestured to me to say more, and people listened quietly as I talked. A few women were fashioning *bilums* from long strands of fiber secured around their toes; others soothed fretful babies. Pirip sat by my chair with her eyes fixed on my face.

"You are Kuma people, aren't you?" I asked, and Gabriel nodded, his brows raised in surprise. "I learned that from the writings of an Australian woman who lived among your people after the war with the Japanese," I explained "I learned about many of your customs, but I know that you want to make changes." Then I mentioned another book that would interest those who read English: *Papua New Guinea, Which Way?* Written by Utula Semana from Morobe Province, it questioned whether PNG would repeat the mistakes that other countries have made or would develop in different ways, involving women in the development. Finally, I asked about the progress of this women's association.

Gabriel, who had been translating our words, was the spokesman—an articulate one, too. Oratory was highly esteemed among the Kuma people.

"You see, there is a Provincial Council of Women; the president is Betty Takip," he said. "Pirip is the treasurer, but she has not seen the books. The Provincial Council has been allocated 20,000 kina to be divided among the districts, but Pirip's group has not received any funds. Unfortunately, funds allocated for women by the national government, and distributed by the provincial government, often do not reach the villages.

"This group must make an application which costs 50 kina, and Betty decides on the applications. There are projects such as chicken raising and piggery—some women are trying to enhance traditional agricultural practices to earn money.

"Women have no voice in the distribution of family resources," Gabriel went on as the women watched him intently, some nodding in apparent agreement. "In the time of Pirip's mother, men were pre-occupied with warfare as well as hunting. Women had autonomy in their own domain. Since warfare has been abolished, men are more involved with family affairs, and they keep women subordinate. They boss women around and control family resources. Women do have access to medical services and education, but only if the man of the family decides it should happen because it involves an expenditure of money. Women are very much burdened."

"And does bride-price continue?" I asked, surprised by Gabriel's insight.

"Yes," said Gabriel, "but that has changed too. It is often presented as cash, and the amounts have risen so much that the government is proposing a bride-price control. Men now view it as the purchase of a woman that entitles the husband to treat her as property." At last I understood why, six years before, Busy Bee and Benjamin made pronouncements that inflamed me: "It costs so much to buy a woman," and "It's only right that a woman should work harder than a man—a bride is so expensive."

"Pirip began her women's work around the time of independence—she was one of the first," Gabriel went on as my gaze connected with Pirip's. She had a smile in her eyes. "She has faced many obstacles—women's allegiances to their own clan groups, male opposition to change, and her own illiteracy. She was not making much progress until her brother, who is a retired policeman, and I gave our support."

"What's your own work?" Bob asked as Gabriel paused.

"I am an educator—I was myself educated at the university. I was in the provincial government until recently, but I lost my office when my party went out of power. I believe that literacy is essential. I have offered to teach the women to read and write."

"That would be wonderful," I said. "I belong to an organization called the Women's International League for Peace and Freedom. I'd like to enroll Pirip as a member so she could receive their English newsletter and learn about women in other parts of the world. But could you teach spoken English first, so that the women could communicate to outsiders like me?" I glanced around the gathering. "For example, I'm not hearing from any of the women here about what they would like to change in their own lives," I said.

But the women were silent until after the men ambled out with Gabriel in the lead. Maybe my comment had prompted the exit, or maybe it was thirst, since he sent a boy off to his trade store/beer hall to buy bottled soft drinks. It was there, he explained to Bob, that the snooker table was entertaining local men. Wisely, Bob didn't tell me that until we were home.

Elizabeth Tuan, a slender young woman who identified herself as a community organizer, turned to me and explained the women's silence: "It is our custom that women do not speak until the men have finished speaking," she said in a soft voice. Then several women drifted away to prepare a *mumu* in our honor, and Pirip and Elizabeth drew closer.

"Pirip would like to make you one of the registered members of her group," Elizabeth told me. "There are thirty women and six men—the men are in the group to assist with construction."

"Thank you, Pirip. That would be an honor," I said, then Elizabeth went on.

"Pirip says this bush house with seven sides was her idea. Many of Pirip's ideas were taken by Betty, and she wonders if Betty might have taken the missing money too. I am working with these women to get a grant of 200 kina."

"I'd like to contribute 200 kina that I've saved from my own work in the States," I told the women. Coincidentally, I had come with this exact amount, dismayed about the Women's Network funds that were apparently stolen. I handed the bills to Pirip, who stuffed them down the front of her smock while the other women still with us exclaimed and smiled broadly.

They tugged and pushed me outside of the house, and I was the target of reaching arms as they put a corona of blossoms on my head and another around my neck. Then, to my surprise and consternation I was lifted into the air by seven women, all of them smaller than I. Amidst a babble of talk and laughter, I was carried completely around the outside of the building while my astonished husband snapped pictures as fast as he could.

When my feet were back on the ground, Elizabeth drew me behind the *haus win*. "Carrying you that way is a custom of ours," she said, and went on talking in a voice just above a whisper. "I am a coordinator—there are two in each province. I try to find out what each association wants and guide them. I try to help them become modern—for example, to build separate pig houses a certain distance from the house for their health, and to learn how to use cooking utensils and eating utensils. And I am trying to encourage them to start on a small project, maybe raising chickens."

But there was no chance to talk about her ideas because Elizabeth and I were surrounded again by milling women, smiling, touching my arms, my cheeks—I felt cradled in their warm embrace. Then Bob and I were led over to where the *mumu* had been served out on banana leaves, and we all sat on the ground, shaded by arching bamboo, and happily munched *kaukau* and roasted corn.

As the light waned, Agua urged us to leave for Mt. Hagen since the highway was unsafe after dark. There could be holdups by *rascols,* and a heightened risk of hitting a pig or a person and incurring deadly *payback.*

But first, Pirip led Bob and me proudly into a rectangular sleeping house—*haus bilong slip*—which would become a guest house for tourists. In the largest of four rooms that were partitioned with split *pitpit* canes, Pirip shyly presented us with gifts: for Bob, a small men's *bilum* to be worn over his shoulder and a cap woven from *cuscus* fur; for me, a gleaming kina crescent and a *bilum* to bring back to the Women's Network.

"Pirip says, your association may decide to keep it, or they may want to sell it," Elizabeth told me.

"I'm sure we'll want to keep it," I said. How could we consider selling this emblem of connection between women?

When we came out, our vehicle had been transformed into a carriage of celebration—the bumpers, mirror, door handles, roof rack were festooned with blossoms and foliage, and on the front fenders two up-thrusting stalks of heliconia would herald our approach. Bob had been garlanded too by now—they sensed his warmth and interest—and the group closed in to say good-bye. When Pirip hugged me tightly again, it was hard to pull away.

Tears stung my eyes the whole way back as every passing car or truck honked a salute to our decorations.

"We decorate the car for important people," Agua explained.

◈ ◈ ◈

Being important felt like a heavy responsibility right then. I had doubts about Elizabeth Tuan's aims—I'd read about "the house-wifization of highland women." Would forks really improve their lives, or only the lives of fork salesmen? And raising chickens could be a fruitless endeavor. Chicken feed could be costly, it often had to be procured from a distant place, and the expense might never be recovered. But I'd stayed silent, hesitating to question Elizabeth's ideas, but also longing to hear more about the group's own goals. Was just having cash a goal in itself?

The cash economy was introduced to New Guinea by Europeans, who first settled along the coasts and outer islands, and needed cheap, compliant labor for their plantations. Fostering wants for manufactured goods was a way to ensure that indigenous workers would stay in their cash-producing jobs, rather than turning back to the independence of agrarian life.

In the highlands now, a cash economy seemed noxious to me, breaking into the elaborate systems of exchange that cemented social ties. And it introduced new inequities. The few who could find cash-paying jobs were men like Benjamin, Paul, and Agua. Was cash improving the nutrition, health, education, or the contentment of women? There was little evidence of that yet.

So was I touching these women's lives in a way that was constructive or not? I was needing to be needed when we first came to Minj in 1983. My daughter and son were grown, my husband was absorbed in a challenging new job, my professional life was once again embryonic, my place in the Upper Valley was undefined. Reaching for connection, I had allied myself with the Kuma's women's longing to enter the modern world, with cash as their passport. Was that passport going to help them or would it cause them harm?

Perhaps travel in the Tari Basin would suggest some answers. We had been learning about customs "in the time of Pirip's mother," as Gabriel put it, but they had been eroded by the modernization flooding Wahgi Valley. Bob and I wanted to plumb traditional life more deeply. Even though different highland groups had developed distinct beliefs, there were common denominators too. And we wanted a broader context in which to understand Pirip's struggles. We were drawn to Tari by stories of deep, enduring tensions between women and men.

Chapter Seven

PARADOX IN HULI LAND

His loins covered by a narrow *laplap,* his muscular buttocks barely concealed by his *as gras,* a worker at Ambua Lodge was guiding a power mower in the crisp morning air. He seemed like an emblem-in-motion, representing the paradoxes in this intriguing land, as Bob and I watched him through the window of our circular bungalow. That was itself a paradox—traditional in style, with woven pandanus walls and a thatched roof, but comfortable beds, electricity, and efficient plumbing.

At 7,000 feet, this wilderness lodge overlooked a stunning panorama of the verdant Tari Basin and jagged mountains beyond. Now part of Southern Highlands Province, the basin was another upland realm that was long unknown to the outside world. Much larger than Wahgi Valley, it revealed itself more slowly to outside eyes. Although an Australian expedition struggled into the populated basin in 1935, no patrol post was established until 1952. Christian missionaries needed several more years to commence their conversion of the Huli people living there, and the Highland Highway didn't snake through the valley until 1981.

◈ ◈ ◈

"There are two answers," said Andrew, our Huli guide, in response to almost every question Bob and I asked him. In Andrew's mind, ancient and modern truths both clashed and coexisted. Even his names reflected the dissonances in his life. "Andrew is my Christian name," he explained. "Kagil is my clan name. My father's name is So."

Andrew was a slender man about five and a half feet tall. Although Huli men were reputed to be volatile and fierce, he seemed gentle, with a wistful aura around his heavily lidded eyes and deep furrows etched in his forehead. It was a look I'd seen among Pirip's people too—forlorn, wistful, bewildered, or something I didn't understand. There was reason for bewilderment among people being catapulted from the age of *as gras* to the age of space suits in just a few decades.

"I was born in a large family," Andrew told us as we set out to explore Tari Basin together. "In many families, only one or maybe two can go to school because of the fees for school supplies and transportation. My family could send me to primary school. In grade six, I took the national examination for high school. Among thirty-five pupils, I ranked number five."

"So you were a fine student," Bob said warmly, but even Andrew's smile was wistful.

"I went to boarding school in Mendi for grades seven, eight, and nine." Mendi was the major town of Southern Highlands Province, located to the southeast of Tari town where our small plane from Mt. Hagen had landed. "But at grade nine I had to drop out because my family did not have the cash—it was 300 or 400 kina for boarding fees, and more for clothing and books and pens. I cried," Andrew said, his eyes misting over.

"It was very hard to find a job. Before, the teachers and police had three years of schooling. When I left school, the government wanted them to finish high school, and even go to university. But my older brother had a car, and he trained as a mechanic. So I became his assistant; I learned to drive and I got my license. Then I got my job as a guide."

With Andrew at the wheel of a four-wheel-drive Toyota, we made a long descent from Ambua Lodge into the populous valley— few Hulis lived up by the lodge because the nights were too cold. It was a bone-jarring descent on the rough highway, but at every turn the landscape rewarded us for the jolts. At roadside, casuarina trees rose high above the gleaming *pitpit,* with whorls of feathery foliage drooping from slender branches. Where trees were sparse, crisply contoured mountains defined the horizon. Where the road dipped low, it crossed tributaries of the Tagari River that scoured out this valley in the hazy past of geology and myth.

We sprayed dust on an endless file of Huli people. Exuberant youths—some in jeans—were striding along with bows over their shoulders and arrows clutched in their hands. Dignified old men in *laplaps* and *as gras* sported crescent-shaped wigs embellished with flowers and feathers; the early Australian explorers marveled at these adornments, and male Hulis have been known as wig-men ever since. But the women, whose grass skirts rustled below shapeless *meri* blouses, were not striding along but trudging, bearing their bulging *bilums*.

Some of the women looked ghostly. White clay had been smeared on their skin, giving it a dull, unhealthy look, and their necks were encumbered with multiple strands of pale grey seeds. "Those are called Job's tears," Andrew explained. "The women are mourning."

Huli women acted as the public carriers of grief when a father, brother, husband, son, or other kinsman died. In past times, a widow needed more than this drab garb of mourning. She needed to display a frenzy of sorrow—sometimes even tearing up her own food gardens—to avoid suspicion that she had caused her husband's death with menstrual contamination or some other poison. A frenzy was less common now, but the widow and other women in the family were expected to keen loudly at the time of death, and to mourn for many months.

We passed neatly built rectangular mounds of earth along the roadside. "Graves?" Bob asked, and Andrew nodded. On top of many of the oblong bases, there were smaller constructions. Some were made of colorful plants and flowers, but one looked like a tiny Christian church with painted white walls, a peaked, corrugated iron roof, and a crucifix above a small door. A yard away, there was a sobering sign: CAR ACCIDENT! Underneath was the victim's name, RINGI NOROBE KOPI.

"All these graves—have all these people been killed on the road?" Bob asked soberly.

"No, but those are the graves of important people," Andrew

told him "It might be a young man killed in an accident, like the last one. But more are young man killed in battle."

"What about children and elderly men?" I asked. "And women?"

"They are buried in the bush," Andrew explained.

"So they're not important!" I wanted to say sarcastically, but I held it back. Andrew would have been perplexed.

"We used to leave bodies on a platform in an open box," he said. "The spirit stays near the body for three or four months, so it is best not to get too close if you walk around the grave. After three or four years, we would take the bones and put them in a special cave. I know a man, when he would have a sickness or a pain— maybe a headache or a pain in his leg—he would take out his grand-mother's bones. He would put the right bone on the part that pained and that would cause healing. Then he would build a new box and put the bones back again. Then the missionaries came and told us it was unhealthy to leave the bodies in the open. We should bury the dead in the ground."

"Do the Huli people want that?" Bob asked. Andrew looked troubled. "Suppose your brother died. One night his ghost might come to you in your dreams. You would feel very sorry, and you would want to hold his bones to be near him again. So maybe after a year, you would dig up his bones."

"What would the Christian pastor say about that?" Bob asked.

"He would not like it," Andrew admitted.

"Would he know?" I asked, since the raised mounds could be penetrated from the side. Andrew was silent for a moment, then he said, "Everyone belongs to a church now, but few obey the rules. Sometimes men even decorate their own bodies with the bones. I will take you to see a Big Man who keeps his uncle's bones in the customary way."

Leaving the Toyota at the roadside, we began walking along a narrow lane, and then through deep trenches between boundary walls twelve to fifteen feet tall. They were earthen walls constructed in sheer vertical planes. Some showed raw soil, as though a giant knife had just sliced them, some were mossy, some overgrown with grasses and vines, some planted on top with trees to hold the soil in place. Many were crowned with wooden spikes. The trenches were used for ambush as well as escape by Huli warriors, and, in the eerie isolation, it was easy to imagine that we might encounter a stealthy warrior, his weapons ready.

Here and there, a plank bridge led across a ditch to the entrance of a homestead—a formidable entrance made of vertical planks sharpened to spikes on top, some stained red and ominously suggestive of blood. A small section of the barrier could be removed, creating an awkward gate.

"Why are the gates so low?" I asked.

"You see, some of the houses have a hole in the floor," said Andrew. "It leads through a tunnel to outside the wall. If the enemy comes, maybe one man would stay and make noises so the enemy thinks there are many inside. That is why gates are low and doorways too. It takes time for the first man to pass through so the ones inside can escape.

"You must never pass through a Huli gate unless you have the owner's consent," Andrew cautioned as he led us, crouching, through a gate and across a large clearing to a thatch-roofed house where the Big Man was standing, glowing with vitality. Over his *laplap* he wore three lengths of woven orange fibers, each with a clump of silky fur at its end. A cassowary bone, sharpened at one end, had been stuck through his belt like a dagger, and a large kina crescent hung below his throat. A fountain of coral raggiana bird of paradise plumage soared above his wig, and golden daisies adorned each side near his ears; both colors were echoed in the daubs of vivid ochres on his face. But the energy he exuded came from more than his exotic adornment. I wished I understood its source.

After he'd exchanged smiles and handshakes with each of us and some words with Andrew, the Big Man led us into the dappled shade of a clump of white-barked trees. There stood a bier, a simple wooden box on stilts, open to the sky and festooned with flowers. The skull and long bones of his uncle lay inside. Cheerfully, the Big Man lifted out the skull, smeared with red ochre in the traditional way, for our inspection.

When the uncle was dying, Andrew explained, he implored the Big Man not to bury him underground in the new way. He feared that his spirit would be imprisoned. In return for that pledge, the dying man promised that his spirit would protect the Big Man's children. That was a special promise since the *dinini*—the ghosts or spirits of the dead—were prone to cause mischief among the living, at least for several months until they passed on to *humbirini andaga*, the distant realm of the dead.

"Do you believe those spirits have the power to cause harm?" I asked Andrew, and he nodded.

"Sometimes I do," he said. "Many people fear the spirits. That's why some like the Christian idea that the spirit goes to heaven where it doesn't cause trouble." He fell silent for a few minutes, then he blurted out, "Nobody *really* knows what happens to the spirit, do they?" Andrew was studying my face intently. "Many new churches have come to Papua New Guinea. Every pastor tells us that his church is teaching the truth. How can we know what really is the truth?"

"Maybe we can't," I said, touched by his trusting candor. It felt like Pirip's trusting reach toward me for help and for answers. "People believe many different things about gods and spirits, Andrew, but nobody really knows for sure."

◈ ◈ ◈

Andrew's worries about spirits played across my mind that night as Bob and I warmed each other in bed. We were nesting like spoons, the backs of my thighs against the fronts of his. Body to body, but what about souls? Did I know as much about his transition as I was learning about the people of PNG? I pulled his arm across my breasts and stroked his golden brown fuzz, the color of *cuscus* fur.

"What was it *really* like for you when we moved?" I asked him.

"Where on earth did that come from?" he asked in surprise. Our move, at least the physical move, had happened over seven years ago.

"Thinking about Andrew and transition, Pirip and transition, you and transition." There was a long silence, then Bob rolled onto his back.

"It was a lot of things," he said slowly. "I didn't find what I'd been told I'd find, so it was like walking down unfamiliar pathways. I felt pretty unsure of myself."

"But you had an instant identity as the new medical school dean. Didn't that help?"

"Sure, but people had different attitudes about a new dean, so it wasn't always the plus you thought it was." Some people hoped he'd be a clone of his predecessor, Bob explained, and some hoped he'd be radically different. "Some people resented the changes I wanted to make, and others were just plain competitive." He was silent again, and I couldn't see his face. His lower lip juts out when he feels sad, like a small boy on the verge of tears.

"I was lonely, too," Bob went on. I wanted to turn toward him but I was afraid of staunching the flow of words. "There wasn't anybody as a sort of mentor I could confide in. I didn't know who was an ally and who wasn't and sometimes I felt kind of betrayed—somebody I'd thought was an ally would pass on things I'd said to him privately."

"You've never talked about it this way before." Bob's words were pounding my solar plexus; I wanted to hug my knees against my chest.

"No, because I was worried about you, you were having a hard time carving out a life for yourself. And I'll tell you now, quite honestly, I was sometimes pretty resentful that you were having such a hard time."

"So because you resented the way I was feeling, you closed off from me, was that it?"

"I guess so. But you seemed pretty closed off from me," Bob said with a flair of irritation. "I was afraid I'd made an awful mistake in accepting the deanship."

"I thought I'd made an awful mistake in agreeing to move after thirty-two years," I said, hearing the edge in my own voice. "I've spent so much time wondering what kept me from telling you flat out that I didn't want to leave New Haven. Maybe I wasn't sure at first; we did quite a job of convincing ourselves the time was right—but then it began to feel unbearable and I couldn't say so."

"But I told you I didn't want to go unless you did too," Bob reminded me.

"I know, and I know you meant it. But your face would light up when you talked about going—you were really turned on by the challenge. It was a weird bind; I didn't want it for me but I did want it for you. I'd have felt mean and selfish if I'd asked you to pass it up—I'd have felt I was letting you down badly.

"Besides, it's hard even to think of myself separately from you; I'm part of you and you're part of me. A lot of women feel that way about their partners."

"Men do too," said Bob.

"You do, but some men aren't so clear about it." Then I noticed the velvet blackness outside the windows. "Well, a lot of new realms opened up in our lives. Being here, for one—that's a huge one. It's kind of strange really—we've been moving from New Haven to New Hampshire by way of New Guinea; I mean understanding what happened to us there by being here."

Chapter Eight

THE ZEST OF WAR

Huli wig-men rushed past us one day as we explored the Tari lanes with Andrew. Garbed in *laplaps* and *as gras*—no jeans today—many had blackened their faces, taking on a menacing mien. They gripped bows that were taller than themselves in one hand, and clutched arrows in the other.

They had an air of excited purpose, but it was disconnected from us. In fact, one man was willing to slow his stride and pose amiably for Bob's camera. In the prime of his life, he had obviously taken time to create an imposing appearance. Flares of plumage— flame red from a raggiana bird of paradise, emerald from a parrot, and ebony from a cassowary—adorned his wig, and a gleaming kina shell almost completely encircled his neck. A broad swathe of black had been painted across his nose and cheekbones, carefully outlined in a scarlet band that also swept around his eyes. He had shaved his beard to expose the center of his chin, and tucked a long black umbrella into the *bilum* knotted diagonally across one shoulder. It was as neatly furled as any umbrella on Regent Street in London— a touch of paradoxical elegance for this Huli dandy with a toe in the modern world.

"What's happening, Andrew?" Bob asked as we walked on.

"A war broke out four months ago," Andrew explained. "These men are on their way to talk about compensation—we call it *pay-back*. But they become very excited. Another fight might break out during the discussions. That is why they are always ready with their weapons."

"Why are their faces painted black?" I asked.

"It is so they cannot be easily identified," Andrew told me. "You see, if it is known who started a war, he must pay compensation for injuries and deaths among those who fight with him, and maybe among his enemies too."

"What usually ends a war?"

"Maybe one side gives up and runs away. Maybe one side offers to pay compensation to the other to keep the war from spreading. Sometimes both sides agree to stop, but that usually does not happen until a Big Man, or several Big Men, come into the discussion and settlements are arranged."

"Do they only use arrows and spears?" asked Bob. "What about guns?"

"Guns are outlawed by the national government—the government is trying to recall all guns that were issued to non-police." Now Andrew led us into a compound where a man was practicing his marksmanship. A brown wig concealed his hair but his beard was grizzled.

"Would he show us how he shoots?" I asked, and Andrew relayed the request. The aging warrior smiled and nodded, and when he crouched to steady himself on the uneven ground, his quadriceps bulged and rippled. He shifted his weight to his leading left leg as his left arm extended to hold the bow. Then, lifting his right elbow high, he pulled the bowstring into an arc deeper than the arc of the bow, while sunlight undulated across the ridges and valleys of his ribs. There was a moment of frozen energy—his body was as taut as the bowstring, as though the entire man might follow the trajectory of the arrow. But the arrow flew through the air alone, landing a hundred yards away.

When Bob and I applauded, the warrior spoke briefly to Andrew.

"He asks if you would like to shoot," Andrew told Bob.

After an instant of hesitation, Bob nodded and accepted the bow that had been carved from black palm traded up from the lowlands. The bowstring was a bamboo strip; Bob guessed it was strung at a tension of thirty to forty pounds.

Bob is a healthy and active man with well-developed shoulders. But when he fitted the arrow to the bow and then grimaced with effort, he could only pull the bowstring back a few inches. And when he released the tension, the arrow failed to soar. It dropped forlornly to the ground. Several men were watching, and they laughed. It wasn't a derisive laugh, it was amiable amusement. They were surely feeling some pride because this Western man couldn't do what they so easily did.

I wasn't sure what the Western man was feeling; he was examining the intricately carved arrows. They had barbs that would embed themselves deep in the flesh. As Bob cautiously fingered the needle-sharp points, one of the watchers limped over on a swollen ankle and pointed toward his thigh. Unwinding a strip of bright blue plastic above his knee, he showed Bob an oozing wound the size of half a dollar, like a bull's eye in the center of insulted flesh. "There are pieces of arrow in there that I cannot get out," he told Bob in English. "The Tari Health Center will remove them, but I must pay cash, so I will try our traditional ways of healing."

"The Tari Health Center gives free medical care but not for injuries from war," Andrew explained.

Today we were only brushed by the zest of war—the glow of vitality that emanated from the warriors striding past. It was a raw maleness, maybe the Iron John that Robert Bly believes is at the core of every man.

◈ ◈ ◈

Conrad Haluma, who began guiding us several days later, had been personally aggrieved.

"My cousin was killed in a war four days ago," he volunteered as we set out across Tari Basin, driving north into Enga Province. While Conrad was away from Tari with other travelers, his house was burned down, along with those of his clansmen. And a car he bought with money earned through his work as a guide was torched as well.

"We're really sorry, Conrad," I said and I meant it even though, at first, he seemed less endearing than Andrew. Conrad was huskier than Andrew and moved with a touch of swagger. Under his bushy mustache, he had a slight smile when he wasn't speaking. At first it looked self-satisfied; later I saw it as tentative and questioning.

As we traveled with Conrad for several days, he told his story again and again. Each time he saw an acquaintance along the road, he stopped and told his story in English, pidgin, or his own Huli language, sounding and looking solemn yet excited. The news of the war was spread through his story, and maybe the telling relieved some of the pressure of sadness, frustration, and fury about the loss.

"What started the war, Conrad?" Bob asked.

"A young man of one clan tried to steal some gold another man found at the new mine in Porgera," he explained. The Porgera mine, north of Ambua, was King Solomon's mine—a strike of gold so pure and bountiful that we'd heard tales of nuggets as big as a fist lying there for the taking. We'd heard that the road to Porgera was unsafe for travel because of holdups by *rascols* who expected to find wealth in any passing vehicle. We'd heard tales of drunken violence, and, across the valley from Ambua at night, we'd seen the lights of a newly built jail.

Most Huli fights erupted out of personal grievances. Disputes about bride-price, war compensation, pig theft, or land encroachment were common. And now they were also about the gleaming metal that has shaped so much of human history.

Conrad was heroic at the wheel. His muscular arms worked constantly as the ever-roughening road coiled through the mountains. The rises were so steep that we passed PMVs (public motor vehicles) that couldn't reach the crests until passengers were unloaded to walk up on their own.

We crossed frothing white rivers, and then we faced an apparent disaster. A huge evergreen tree lay directly across the road. Bob and I groaned, imagining ourselves in a similar plight on an interstate at home, traffic backed for miles, horns blaring as drivers waited impatiently for the highway department to arrive with heavy mechanical equipment.

Conrad seemed frantic, twisting the 4WD off the road in an effort to bypass the tree, slamming it into reverse and then fruitlessly trying other routes. He feared that this was a *rascol* ambush, I suspected; at the moment, I was too curious to be afraid.

But neither his scenario nor ours was enacted today. A dozen men materialized from the surround and, with bush knives and axes, they opened a passage in less than ten minutes. As we drove on, Conrad relaxed and soon he volunteered another story. Sitting next to him up front, I waited out every pause as he fitted together the shards of memory.

"I saw my first white man in 1963 when I was a boy of eight. First I saw footprints, they were the prints of feet that had no toes. Another day I saw a man with white skin. I told my mama and she said that because the man was white and had no toes, he must be a spirit. She told me not to look or else he might steal my spirit away.

"It was a missionary who came to the region of my father," Conrad remembered. "All the people were frightened because they thought he was a spirit of the dead. I wanted very much to see him, but my mama said if I went I must go with many others. So after some time, I would creep to his house to see him. I counted his fingers, and I thought his hair was made from cornsilk.

"One day the priest saw me, and he gave me a bucket and told me to get water from the river. Then he asked me to be his houseboy. At first, when the priest went away, I would go to the place where he left his excreta." Conrad looked at me inquiringly, wondering whether this was all right to tell, and I nodded, suspecting what was coming. I was more stirred than repelled by his search for an elemental human linkage. "I would put a stick down into his excreta and bring it up to smell. And I found that it was just the same as mine. So then I stayed with him for six years."

◈ ◈ ◈

Our destination was Kaiap Orchid Lodge, perched on a 9,000 foot ridge in the cloud forest above Wabag, Enga's principal town. Our small, unheated room was frigid, but the welcome from Peter Piawen, the local owner, was warm. And when I groped my way down to the communal washroom at two A.M (the generator went off at nine), I saw Peter dozing in the firelit lounge, alert to any intrusion that might threaten his guests—a dawn raid, for example. Indeed, we were soon to learn that one came close to where we slept.

After an enchanted morning spotting birds and examining the rare orchids that Peter gathered from the forest for propagation, Bob and I decided to walk down the steep, rutted, four-mile road that we'd lurched up in the 4WD the afternoon before. Here there were no boundary walls, and we passed thatched dwellings along the ridge, responding to friendly greetings from householders and people hurrying down the road. Most of the men were carrying weapons; some small boys were too.

"A war broke out this morning," an English-speaking passerby explained enthusiastically. "All the people are going down to watch."

"Can we watch, too?" Bob asked.

"Yes, come with me." As we tried to keep pace beside him, the excited young man told us the details.

Two weeks ago, a woman from this side of the river below the ridge went over and talked to a man on the other side. His wife became jealous and stabbed the visitor, inflicting a serious wound. The brothers of the injured woman demanded compensation. It was not forthcoming. Instead, aggrieved at the woman who had intruded, men came across the river early this morning, crept up the steep slope, and set fire to a house in which sixteen people were sleeping.

"To kill them?" Bob asked, looking horrified.

"To make them come out. You see, we use *pitpit* for the roofs of our houses and it makes them very strong. People try to make their roof strong because, when there is a war, men try to tear off the roof to get to the people inside. It is *tambu* to burn people inside their houses, so warriors have to pull the men out and then they can chop them to pieces with their axes." I shuddered at the savage image, but that had not happened this morning. Rather, the men came out fighting and helped the women and children escape. Now war was raging down by the river.

As we rushed over to the edge of the ridge where spectators had gathered, the charred remains of five torched dwellings came into view. There was commotion among the people here—they shifted around, peering downward, talking in loud, staccato voices. Surges of yelling boiled up from below where the warriors were fighting, almost invisible among the trees. We saw flashes of movement, but we could only imagine the scene—the bowmen crouched and taut, seeking the best target fifty yards away, others hurling their spears at the nearest enemy body.

"We use *pitpit* for spears, too—I had a spear in my side," our escort volunteered proudly. He pulled up his T-shirt to show us a small, round scar just below his ribs. "I pulled it very hard and it came out. Then when the blood was thick and turned to milk, I went to a medicine man. He took a small piece of *pitpit,* a different kind. He said some magic words, then he sucked the wound and so it got well."

Below, four men had already been injured, one with an axe and three with spears. Yet as close as we now were to the violence, I felt no sense of menace, nor, apparently, did the dozens of other watchers. As Busy Bee had told us in the Wahgi Valley, highland warfare was selective; only known enemies were at risk.

As we sat on the grassy verge, hearing the shouts of ferocious combat, bewilderment washed over me. "Civilized" countries make war with bombs and missiles that mutilate the innocent as well as the guilty, helpless civilians as well as armed warriors. In high-tech war, it is not *tambu* to burn people inside their houses. Is it moral to urge people like these, whose aggression is still channeled, into our modern ways?

And what about my efforts for Pirip?

◈ ◈ ◈

Ironically, our own war impeded those efforts.

In August of 1990, Saddam Hussein's forces invaded Kuwait. Condemning this "naked aggression" and encouraging Saudi Arabia to request our military presence, President Bush began mobilizing our troops. By the autumn equinox, Bob's and my suspicions coalesced.

Yes, the invasion of Kuwait was atrocious and the United Nations embargo on trade with Iraq was essential. But the immense buildup of US military forces in Saudi Arabia—with its docudrama label of Operation Desert Shield—suggested an inexorable momentum toward war. A war that could deflect our national attention from a soaring deficit, a savings-and-loan scandal, homelessness, child abuse, rampant crime, drug addiction, AIDS, poisoned air, water, and soil. It could focus our outrage on villains outside our society rather than those within.

In November, our president upped the ante. There would be half a million US troops in the gulf. Now my sleep was fitful and laced with dread. Our son was too old for this call to arms, but what was coming next? There were murmurs about World War III.

Even in my helpless terror I felt implacable. I would not sacrifice my beloved son to a war that made no sense to him, to us, to many others. I would hide him or disguise him or flee with him to Papua New Guinea. I would take him to a men's house near Minj where there was a secret room.

During the last two weeks of the year, in spite of holiday travels and school vacations, more than 1,200 people in the Upper Valley united in urging President Bush to continue economic and diplomatic sanctions against Iraq but to "STOP THE RUSH TO WAR!" They were carpenters and professors, farmers and physicians, artists and shopkeepers. They were octogenarians and teenagers and thirtysomethings. They were veterans of three wars and pacifists. They were Christians, Jews, and agnostics. But we couldn't halt the juggernaut.

Operation Desert Shield became Operation Desert Storm in Baghdad on January 17th when the bombing began.

Within days, our press raised vexing questions:

Why had the US approved of France and the USSR supplying Saddam Hussein with deadly weapons during the Iraq-Iran war—weapons that were now being used against our own troops?

Why, on July 25th, did our ambassador to Iraq respond to Hussein's expressed grievance about Kuwait by saying that the United States had "no opinion" about Arab-against-Arab conflicts, allowing Hussein to believe we would not intervene in hostilities against Kuwait?

Why did President Bush assure us on August 8th that our mission in Saudi Arabia was entirely defensive, and then shift to an offensive stance on November 8th while Congress was in recess?

Why did our leader commit so many troops to the Gulf that we could not financially maintain them long enough to allow economic sanctions against Iraq to work?

I had ghastly questions of my own:

Was President Bush's urge to make war as intense as Saddam Hussein's? As intense as a volatile Huli wig-man's?

Was this war our president's rite of manhood—this leader with awful powers who exhorted our troops to "kick a little ass"?

The missiles were streaking through the sky. After the first show of power, some of our compatriots called for a cease-fire. Our leaders were deaf. Images of apocalyptic violence pervaded every household with TV. Excited men surfed between war scenes and football scenes on Sunday afternoons. My male clients, with varying degrees of shame, confided their exhilaration; some had erections as they watched the soaring projectiles.

The media coverage was so tightly censored, the images so carefully crafted that the watchers could cheer with no tug of compassion, no drag of guilt. As the missiles pierced the sky and the "smart bombs" fell, they seemed to make precise surgical penetrations. Men, women, and children weren't really dying, the military suggested, only tanks. Dying tanks don't scream. Dying tanks don't bleed.

And if a bomb did fall on a shelter or a school, well, that was only collateral damage.

Late that month, I went to a national meeting of mental health professionals. It was about suicide and other violence, and had been planned a year before. But now the war was bearing witness to the central theme of the conference: The United States had developed a "culture of destruction."

A suicide occurred every twenty minutes. 35,000 were confirmed each year but it was believed that up to 100,000 actually took place.

There were 25,000 murders every year, half erupting out of domestic violence. Around four million women were beaten by male partners each year, and 800,000 were raped.

For two days we were pounded by ugly realities about our country, which the US Senate Judiciary Committee would later declare the most violent in the developed world.

In that horrifying context, we were told that pilots on the US aircraft carrier *John F. Kennedy* were shown pornographic films before leaving on combat missions. This was an Associated Press report published in the *Washington Post*, after initial censorship by the military because it was "too embarrassing." It should have been embarrassing. Among those very young men, sexual arousal was being used as a spur to deadly violence. It was being fused with violence, rather than with affection and concern. How could that not spill over into civilian life?

Toxic machismo was running rampant.

During the war's final days, our son went into a store where a TV newsman was announcing that twenty-eight US soldiers had been hit by a Scud missile. They were dead.

"Think how sad their families must feel," the shopkeeper sighed.

"For sure," Doug agreed. "But think how sad the families of 100,000 dead Iraqi soldiers are feeling too." There was a heavy silence.

"You know, I never thought of that," the woman said in a troubled voice. Why would she have thought of that when TV created the illusion of a war without anguish? It was docudrama, not reality.

But it had been a bloody slaughter. At least 200,000 Iraqis had died, and more children than that were expected to die for want of medicine, food, drinkable water, and electricity. Their hospitals, homes, and roads had been pounded into rubble.

Yet Saddam Hussein still swaggered around.

I wanted to go back to Papua New Guinea. I needed reminders that there were other ways of being human. Non-tech ways. Ways we might reclaim.

I needed to go back to Papua New Guinea. I wanted to find Pirip and say, "Dear sister, please slow down."

◈ ◈ ◈

We drove again toward Minj in March, 1992, this time with serious misgivings. My letters to Pirip had been unanswered and Paul, our driver, said his agency had been unable to contact her. But when we arrived at the lane into her homestead, Kuru, her husband, walked out. He laughed and shouted and hugged me, and held my hand a long, long time.

Then came daughter Ruth with a son of her own. Flickers of surprise, delight, and dismay chased each other across her face.

"Mama Pirip did receive your letters and she wants so much to talk to you, but she thought you were coming on a different date. She's not here." Sharing a heavy disappointment, we settled under the trees to catch up on news. Chris, Ruth's husband, and Kuru joined us.

"There's been trouble in our family," Ruth told us soberly. "My sister Gertrude was beaten by her husband—he said he would cut her throat with an axe or shoot her." Oh God, here too, I thought. "They'll go to court next month to try for a divorce."

"Divorce? What about the bride-price? Can your family pay it back?"

"It wasn't an arranged marriage," Ruth explained. "There was no bride-price because the man couldn't raise it."

"Is Gertrude staying with Pirip?" I asked, and Ruth nodded.

"Until the trouble, Gertrude and her husband stayed together at night, just as the church teaches," Chris explained. "Ruth and I do that too. But Kuru is a traditional man. He goes up to the men's house at night and then spends his days supporting Mama Pirip's work with the women."

"How's that progressing?" I asked. Chris frowned.

"The local women's organization declined after you were here in 1989," he said. "The husbands objected to the organization and there was fighting among the women. Some of the women lost trust in Pirip." That flooded me with troubling doubts. Had I played a part in that loss of trust? Had the lost or stolen $500 played a part? But Chris's voice broke into my worries.

"Later that year there was a *payback* raid and many local homes were burned. The men went away and the women followed."

"Ohhh." I was relieved; a clan war was not my doing. But what bitter irony; war had unraveled Pirip's relationship to local people while another war was unraveling my relationship to my country.

"Mama Pirip hasn't given up," Ruth declared as we gathered ourselves to leave, and there were tears in all our eyes as we said good-bye.

"Damn, damn, damn," I muttered under my breath as we drove away, frustrated at the frenetic pace of our lives, shaped by times and dates and schedules. Pirip would be disappointed once again. And besides, I'd missed her warm, wet, welcoming hug—that elemental skin-to-skin affection. It was heady stuff, feeling so intensely wanted.

I tried to calm myself by reflecting about Kuru—the paradox of his coming down from the men's house each morning to support his wife's effort to change women's lives. Did feeling secure in his male domain protect him from feeling threatened by her aims? Was staying with women at night breeding tensions among other men, such as Gertrude's husband? Was sexual arousal exploding in violence, as it was intended to do on the USS *John F. Kennedy?*

Maybe revisiting the Hulis would help unravel the riddles. We were booked on a flight to Tari the next morning.

Chapter Nine

MAKING MEN

Andrew seemed to share our pleasure at being together again in Tari, and we were soon deep in conversation. I mentioned that men and women in Wahgi Valley were staying together at night nowadays, and asked if that was true in Tari Basin too.

"Yes, some Christian men and women live together now," he said. "I share my room with my wife; I have to take care of her because she left her mother and father to marry me. But many still live in the traditional way. I will show you."

As we joined in the flow of Huli people, a man who looked ancient approached us in a narrow lane, staggering under a load of *kaukau*.

"A *man* with a heavy load?" I blurted out my surprise.

"He wants to carry his own food," Andrew explained. "He likes that better than having his daughter carry it for him." Gallantry? No. That was dread. Having the daughter carry the *kaukau* would be unsafe because her secretions might contaminate the food and cause the old man's death.

"Would he be taking the food to his village?" Bob asked.

"Huli people do not live in villages," said Andrew. "A family group lives in a homestead inside their boundary wall." He led us into a large homestead, divided between the father and mother's land, and the land of their daughter and her husband. Within each couple's realm, there were houses for women and houses for men— all were ground-hugging dwellings similar to Wahgi Valley houses. Near the daughter's home, a small building housed the pigs.

"It was the custom for the pigs to live in the women's houses," Andrew told us. "But when the missionaries and health officers came, they said that was not healthy."

"Where are the people who live here, Andrew?" I asked. Now, at midday, the buildings seemed to be empty.

"They may be at market or they may be working in other gardens. There are always parts of the gardens that are resting; the pigs feed there, and they fertilize the soil," our guide explained. He pointed out the circular mounds in which *kaukau* was grown—a traditional design that promoted drainage during heavy rains. Nearby, there were corn, taro, pumpkins, greens, bananas, and legumes that, with small amounts of animal protein, completed the diet—similar to the traditional Kuma fare.

There was an irony here. The sweet potato, *kaukau,* was probably brought to New Guinea by Malay traders in the sixteenth century—it had been taken to Malaysia from South America by Spanish and Portuguese explorers. So for at least four hundred years, the long-lived Huli people had been eating the "heart-healthy" diet that US cardiologists had just begun promoting.

"Do men and women work together at all?" I asked as we walked on.

"In some families they work together in the gardens, although not to harvest the food. In some families they never cross into each other's gardens," he told us. "They see each other in the market. But they should not look directly at each other's eyes unless they are angry. They should turn their heads away a little while they talk."

"When a man and his wife want to make a baby, they should go into the bush. But not too often," Andrew went on earnestly, "or the man will become weak and his life will be short." We heard the echo of Benjamin's Kuma voice. Like other highland men, the Hulis believed that the supply of semen was finite. To squander it meant to squander a man's vitality.

"It's strange, but you used to hear that sort of thing in the States, too," Bob murmured as we walked through the gardens out of Andrew's earshot. He referred to male athletes being warned by their coaches not to have sex the night before a major game. A crucial energy could be dispelled.

But, for the Hulis, there was a deadly danger—contracting *agali.* This dreaded condition was believed to involve a blackening and twisting of a man's intestines, expressed in abdominal pain, black diarrhea, backache, headache, and weakness in the neck. As the disease advanced, the intestines became so tangled that the colon would burst and death ensued.

This horror, it was thought, was the result of untimely exposure to a woman's "heat" in intercourse. Any occasion except the four days in the middle of her monthly cycle was untimely. The closer to the menstrual period the sex took place, the greater the danger became. And it was intense in the months after childbirth, and near menopause too.

"Sex seems most dangerous when women aren't very fertile," I said to Bob. "Sex is only for making babies—that's the message."

"I wonder if that came from Christian missionaries," Bob mused.

"I'm not so sure," I answered, suspecting that Christian warnings against "carnal pleasure" meshed with what local people already believed. I reminded Bob that when the first anthropologist settled here in the 1950s, males and females were living separate lives.

"Huli morality was already strict, maybe because people thought female sexuality was too powerful. The Hagen and Kuma people did too. But I've read some Huli myths that give clues about the basis. I'll tell you about them tonight."

Noticing that we were deep in conversation, Andrew had stayed at a distance. But now we joined him again.

"Do men have more than one wife?" I asked him.

"Some do," Andrew admitted. "Then the wives live in different parts of the valley."

A marriage took place in stages. First, the chosen bride was escorted to her prospective mother-in-law's house, while the groom remained at his own. For four days and four nights, the couple had to keep themselves awake and stay outdoors while the birds were singing, or else their union would be barren—no babies would be born. On the fifth day, some fertile land was cleared for their gardens, and they could start growing food.

But up to nine months went by before the marriage was consummated. Before that event, the man sacrificed a pig, imploring the spirits to protect him against contamination. And he poured oil from a special tree over his wife's vulva to cleanse it and prepare it for his entrance. Then the couple could try to "make a baby."

"After children are born, where do they live?" I asked Andrew.

"The girls live with the mother until they marry," he said. "But the boys, only until they are about six years old. They go back and forth between mother and father until they are eight or nine, and then they go away from the mother completely. When they are maybe ten, or maybe later, they go into the bush to grow their hair."

The hair was kept moist with dew, Andrew explained, but it was not washed, so when the boy came out of the bush his hair was brown with dust, not black. But before then, the hair grew for three or four months between cuttings, and it took three or more cuttings to make a proper wig. An older man cut off the hair and took it to a wig-maker who made a brown wig for every day and a black one for ceremonies. Then the wig-maker worked in mosses and feathers, and, finally, he bound it all together with spider web.

"Spider web? That looks so fragile," I said.

"It's not," said Bob. "Very high tensile strength." Then he turned to Andrew. "Can the boys find enough food while they're in the bush?"

"While the hair is growing, older men—bachelor men—bring food to the boys."

"Why bachelors?" I asked.

"Because they are pure," said Andrew with calm conviction.

◈ ◈ ◈

That evening, after a savory meal in Ambua Lodge, Bob and I snuggled under the blankets in our chilly cabin, surrounded by books and notes. It had never before seemed special that he felt safe lying close to my body. But now it did, as my thoughts turned to the Huli men who didn't feel safe near their women. I was puzzling out loud about the origins of their dread. There were several Huli myths—*mana*—which portrayed the drama of sexuality and creation.

Honabe, a female deity, was the first inhabitant of the land. Since fire had not yet been created, she cooked her food by the heat of her own genitals. Timbu, a male deity, found her and was aroused by the sight of those genitals, glowing red. He mated with Honabe and, over time, she gave birth to five male deities—Korimogo, Helabe, Piandela, Ni, and Helahuli, the progenitor of the Huli people—and one female deity, Hana. And later, seven other deities, the first bird, and the first possum were born in Honabe's menstrual discharge.

In this tale, menstruation and fertility were linked. And the Hulis still believed that menstrual blood and semen combined to form the fetus. So why was menstruation so imbued with danger?

Some Huli myths conveyed the idea that males had control over female sexuality. For example, in a different version of the Honabe myth, Timbu's penetration during intercourse extinguished the fire in Honabe—the heat that allowed her to cook her own food. And another myth recounted that the female vulva was actually created by a male, who then succumbed to its lure.

"The story goes like this," I told my drowsy husband.

Hana, Honabe's daughter went to the forest one day, and when she thought nobody could see her, she rubbed her body against the trunk of a tree. But her brother, Ni, was watching. After she had left one morning, he went into the forest. He inserted a sharp stone into the tree trunk she used, placing it so that she couldn't see it. When Hana came back to the tree to rub herself, her flesh was gashed by the stone, and this gash formed her vulva. When she stopped bleeding, Hana went back to the women's house. On the way, she met Ni, who had been following her. She told him what had happened, and when Ni saw the wound, he was sexually aroused and mated with his sister. Then they were both very much ashamed. To avoid having to face their mother, Honabe, Ni and Hana rose up to the sky, where he became the sun and she became the moon.

Each male took control of the female and then lost control of himself—so the stories suggested. Timbu was aroused by the glowing vulva, Ni by the bloodied vulva, and both succumbed to its lure.

"There seems to be a link between female genital bleeding and sexual arousal in these stories." I was still pondering out loud. "It makes me think of women in the States who've told me they feel horny just before their menstrual periods, and sometimes during them too."

That same connection was described in studies of sexuality in the United States—by Kinsey first, then Masters and Johnson. There was even evidence of a physical link between heightened libido and menstruation—hormonal shifts and changes in blood circulation in the sex organs. Honabe's "glowing red genitals" sounded a lot like the "vasocongestion" and "engorgement of the genitalia" our scientists wrote about less poetically.

"I wonder if Huli women feel sexy around the time of their periods, too, or if Huli men think of them that way," I mused.

"But you're talking about female arousal," Bob said sleepily. "How does the male fit in?"

"Hey, was that intentional?"

"Was what?"

"That pun."

"Pun?" When Bob's blue gaze looks that angelic, I know he's putting me on. I decided not to rise to the bait.

"Well, think of Ni. He was excited by Hana's bleeding." Now I tried for a coherent explanation. Could it be that sexual desire in both Huli men and women was kept under control by the ideology that Andrew expressed? Sex was only for making babies—and increasing clan size. So sex with a woman during her infertile days would be wasteful, squandering a man's semen. If women felt more sexy near their periods, and if men found their sexiness attractive, then it was easy to see why a menstruating woman was taboo.

While we—mostly I—had been talking, a moon had risen in the ebony sky outside our cabin.

"D'you think that's Hana, trying to shed some light on my musings?" I asked Bob. But there was a long silence from him. Then a muffled snore.

◈ ◈ ◈

We were curious about the forests—or "bush"—in which manhood was shaped, so one day we trudged up toward the 9,000 foot height of Tari Gap—an alpine tundra between towering peaks—where Huli men gathered golden everlasting daisies to decorate their wigs. Joseph Tano was our guide. He was heavily muscled, with skin so dark that his pink fingernails had a luminescent glow, and his short hair and full beard were as dense and black as the forest under thickening clouds.

Along the way, I thought I saw bloodied hand prints on the bark of several trees. "Those are painted signs," Joseph assured me. "It means *tambu*—keep out." No people were living up here, but every square foot of rain forest was privately owned.

"Can we walk in?" Bob asked. "Yes, I know where," Joseph said. Most landowners would give permission for others to pass through their land, or even stay briefly, he explained, as long as there was no hunting or harvesting the fruits of the bush.

"He might even give permission for a friend to cut down one tree—maybe a pandanus. That's our most valuable tree because we use the wood for building houses; we eat the fruits and nuts. Or we might dry the fruit and sell it in the market. Then another man will buy it, boil it, and eat it." We'd seen this awkward-looking tree, with its stiff fronds and stilt roots, in lowland and highland alike.

"The landowners go into the bush for hunting," Joseph continued.

"What kind of game?" Bob asked. They hunted wild pigs, Joseph told us, and marsupials, some unique to PNG. And the men hunted birds, including the ferocious cassowary we had seen at the Baiyer River Sanctuary.

"The men go alone, or in groups," Joseph explained, "and they stay for three or four months. They take *kaukau*, enough for several weeks. They hunt, they gather pandanus nuts and many kinds of mushrooms, and they find special mosses to cool their skin." An hour later Joseph offered us some moss, which felt blissfully like sponge that had been dipped in an icy stream. "If they are a long way from a river or pool, they can suck some water from this moss."

Now Joseph turned directly into a morass of vegetation that seemed to writhe like a late–Van Gogh landscape. This was a hunting trail, he said, but it was invisible to us. He led the way through moss-draped oaks and beeches that soared into the sky, arching clumps of bamboo, lacy tree ferns as tall as our mountain ash at home, and nameless vines twisting, creeping, hooking, scrambling toward the sun.

We swung past the sturdy, woody vines that are called lianas, slipping on clay that was slimy from last night's showers, stumbling over roots hidden in the leaf-strewn forest floor, and slithering under fallen branches. "Sorry," Joseph said when we got tangled in growth that he had slid through smoothly.

"I can't hear so well in one of my ears," he told Bob, and he often turned his head as though reaching for sound. A rain forest pulses with a cacophony of noises, but even with his loss of hearing, Joseph discerned each strand in the auditory tangle—he named each birdcall, knew the clicks, hums, buzzes, and whistles of fruit bats, frogs, and insects, and, by following a small cheep unnoticed by us, led us to a tiny brown possum scampering on the branch of a tree.

Joseph listened, he looked, he smelled—breaking off a length of fern from time to time and sniffing it to find evidence of the passing of man or beast—while we followed in a state of total trust. He pointed to glistening white blossoms of rhododendron that grew on moss high in the trees. He spotted tiny orchids nestled in craggy bark—crimson, orange, gold, salmon, or lavender, with petals that were rounded or tubular, contorted or frilled. Many gave off a sweet perfume.

We trod very lightly, fearing that the pressure of each boot would snuff out life. We trod very slowly because there was a riot of growth to see and touch. We paused at fallen logs that expressed the power of regeneration: From the decaying wood, ferns, lichens, and mosses had emerged in sprays, tufts, or daisy shapes; they were prickly, softly fuzzy, or velvety smooth. I wished I knew a ritual that could express my awe.

"Are there spirits in the forest?" I asked Joseph.

"Yes," he said. "Most people believe in both good and bad bush spirits, even Christian people. Educated people, maybe less so." Joseph, who designated himself as a "flora and fauna specialist," had two dimensions of education. From boyhood, he'd been absorbing knowledge about his habitat through his five highly developed senses, and from the teachings of his elders. In studies at the University of Papua New Guinea he'd learned to organize that knowledge into western categories of thought, and he designated that as education.

Had he been taught to doubt his traditional beliefs—to question the existence of the Huli spirits that inhabited the deep pools, caves, and trees? I longed to ask, but the risk of embarrassing him was too high.

"Well," I said, "we're educated and we believe. If a spirit is an energy, a life force, how could we not believe that this forest is a spiritual place?" Joseph looked uncertain, so I returned to familiar ground.

"Are there sacred places in the bush?" I was thinking of the *kebanda*—the places of origin where the ancestor of each clan emerged from the earth, and where rituals were still practiced.

"Yes, there are sacred places, but they are deep in the bush. They are very hard to get to." There was no question of approaching one today—we heard that in his tone of voice. Then he paused at a barely perceptible clearing.

"A father takes a boy into the bush to show him where he could build a little house for hunting when the father dies—a place like this in the father's land. He shows him the boundaries of his land, and the markers for those boundaries—we often use pandanus trees for markers. The father teaches him how to hunt and fish, how to make bows and arrows for hunting and for war, how to fight in a war, and customs that men must know—how you treat a lady and how you make a baby in the bush."

"Sometimes there are bad things in women's bodies that make them unhealthy," Joseph confided to Bob while I was coiling myself around a tree, looking at a cluster of tiny scarlet orchids. "Boys must be taught how to make themselves pure. Some go into the bush alone and stay for maybe eighteen months, but many enter a bachelor house. *Ibagiyanda,* it is called."

"They still exist?" Bob asked. Andrew had mentioned that briefly.

"Yes. There are still many bachelor houses, maybe twelve. They are deep in the bush."

◈　◈　◈

On another day, Conrad took us to the grounds of a bachelor cult. We approached along a narrow dirt road that led also to the Catholic mission high school—a boarding school for youths from miles around. But before reaching that, Conrad parked our rugged vehicle, and we started walking through a trench between high, earthen walls.

We turned and turned again, following bobbing clumps of feathers and leaves. Or so it seemed. A lean man walked steadily, his head engulfed in gleaming cassowary plumes, his back bare except for a spray of *as gras*. We followed him through an open gate into a fenced enclosure where two elderly bachelors were waiting. Waiting? Indeed, because without advance arrangements, two foreigners, one a woman, would never have been admitted. A fee had been paid, we surmised.

The men were a marvelous sight. One held his head high under a coal-black wig, a crescent as crisply shaped as a new moon. The breastplate of a superb bird of paradise—iridescent blue—was centered on the wig, and silky, coral plumage from the raggiana bird of paradise swayed above. The bachelor's stern face was masked with marigold pigment bisected by a vertical line of scarlet, and he had thrust a large cluster of feathers in his bark belt, accenting his manhood.

The breastplate of a red, yellow, and black lorikeet was centered in the rounded brown crescent of the other man's wig, and several long tail feathers from the ribbontail bird of paradise quivered high above. A pair of menacing wild boar tusks curved below his throat.

"Conrad, do the men choose the feathers of special birds for special reasons?" I asked, feeling a surge of sympathy for the exquisite birds that had once soared free. We had seen several as we walked up to Tari gap.

"No, there is no special meaning; they use whatever they like. This is a real *ibagiyanda,*" Conrad went on, and I had the eerie sense that my unspoken thoughts were known—it happened often in New Guinea. Just then, I felt as though we were sliding both forward and backward through slippery time; what *was* and what *is* seemed separated by a permeable membrane, and I wasn't sure what was past and what was present.

"There are still maybe four or six," Conrad said. Joseph had said twelve and the actual number probably wasn't known. "There are six boys here now; they are far away in the bush. They pay a fee, maybe 200–300 kina or pigs, which cost 200–300 kina each. They may pay less. They stay for a year or more, and they must not leave the *ibagiyanda.* If they do go out, the teacher keeps the fee, but the boy must go away from the house.

"The most important thing is cutting the hair and making the wigs. And while the boy is there he learns how to take care of his body and how to clean himself with magic water. When he has completed his time, the leader of the *ibagiyanda* shows him his flaws. Maybe he will point to something on the boy's chest and say that could have been caused by adultery, or that the boy might have talked to a lady, or eaten food prepared by a lady. The boy is supposed to confess, like in the Catholic church. He is healed by confession."

"Was confession expected before the missionaries came?" Bob asked, but Conrad wasn't sure. "Later on," he continued, "the boys may return as bachelor men for more learning. One man came here five times. The boys learn about fighting and how to talk to girls. They learn magic spells, and they learn about medicines for the body."

As he talked, haunting music had floated out of the forest, and now another elder strolled into the clearing playing a panpipe—a cluster of hollow reeds cut to varying lengths. "He is the chief bachelor," Conrad murmured.

A huge crescent-shaped wig massed with golden everlasting daisies cradled the old man's head. It was rimmed with fluffy white feathers, and a cluster of black cassowary plumes erupted from the middle. A yellow line defined the center of the man's high, sloping forehead and traveled down his nose—this was clay from Mt. Ambua that soared above Tari Gap—and his black beard was fringed with yellow. He had thrust a slender reed through his nasal septum, and a gleaming kina shell hung on his chest. His aging belly bulged slightly above his fiber and feather *laplap,* and his *as gras* was a fresh, bright green. A dagger of cassowary bone was poised at his hip.

He must have heard Conrad's words because he chimed in, using his *ples tok,* his local language, and Conrad translated.

"The chief says that boys are taught, 'Your wife is not your toy. She is not to play with every day. She is for making baby.'"

The elder led us to a small garden, where special plants were growing. These were bog iris, a secret plant that women must not know about or see. A Western woman, I'd already realized, didn't fit into the highland category of woman, so it violated no taboo for me to know and see.

It was the elder who tended these plants, and now he showed how he would perform ritual magic. Sprinkling water over the plants—in an actual ceremony he would sprinkle pig's blood—he chanted so urgently that the veins in his neck swelled alarmingly. His chin raised high, he called to the spirits of the mountains and the rivers, and invoked their special powers.

"Each plant belongs to one boy," the elder said after he had caught his breath. "When a boy leaves the house, he can take his plant. If you miss one rule of the cult, your plant will die. If you have thoughts of mothers and girls, it will die." He was silent for a moment, and then the staccato speech began again.

"The chief says, 'A boy can take a special grass when he is ready to go out,' Conrad explained. 'The boy can use it under his arm to attract a girl. He can roll it into a cigarette and smoke it and that bewitches the girl. He can mix it with paint for his body decoration—his *bilas*—to make the color brighter.'"

Bob was frowning and I was bewildered by the paradox: The bog iris enforced a boy's chastity, but another plant strengthened his sex appeal. I didn't have words to sort that out, and now the elder was sauntering away from the garden.

"You people spend a lot of money to see our little customs," he said with a piercing look at Bob. "I used to see people come back here, and since white people look alike, I thought it was the same people. I travel to two, three other countries. I saw lots of white people. I cannot remember their faces. Before, I thought the sky and mountains meet together and no people were beyond. When you people come we know there are other people beyond. A few years ago, a man came and sat with me and asked many questions about our customs." The elder talked on, and Conrad turned to us.

"The chief thinks he may die soon," he said soberly. "He does not want to share his knowledge with younger men."

My rising question, "Why not?" felt like a wrongful intrusion, and I held it back. And I stifled my urge to plead: "Don't try to seal away the past, it doesn't work." The choice was his to make. But I left sadly, with a sense of impending loss.

"Do you think travelers help your people or harm them?" I asked Conrad as we walked away.

"It helps us very much," he said. "It gives jobs for those who work in the lodges, and for the guides. And it helps us to keep our traditions alive." A strange contradiction, this seemed—urging traditional people into the modern world and yet supporting their ancient customs. But their response had been pragmatic. By protecting and yet exposing some of their traditions, they gained access to the cash economy and the goods of the industrialized world. Some males did, at least. And wasn't that what I had intuitively been encouraging Pirip to do? Wasn't her *haus win* an emblem of tradition in the midst of change?

Chapter Ten

"WE ARE THEIR SISTERS, THEIR MOTHERS"

What could it be like to be a Huli woman—a woman whose sexual self was desired yet dreaded by men—a woman whose secretions could expose a man to deadly pollution?

"Is there a way I could meet with some English-speaking Huli woman?" I asked Maryanne who, with her husband, managed Ambua Lodge.

"Why don't you talk to Maria?" she proposed. "She's on our staff here—she cleans the cabins. Just once before she had a chance to talk to a visitor, and she loved doing it."

"Sounds fine," I said. "Is she single or married?" Maryanne hesitated.

"Well, I suppose Maria's not actually married because her husband hasn't finished paying bride-price. Maria met him at the Catholic mission where she was working, and they fell in love. I expect they'll have a Catholic ceremony when the bride-price is paid."

Two evenings later, I met Maria Thomas Nogho, who was about five feet tall and buxom. Her heart-shaped face, under a high crown of wiry black hair, seemed echoed in the motif on her T-shirt—a scarlet heart bisected by a white crucifix, with JESUS imprinted above. Yet the imprint of tradition showed up, too, in faint blue tattoos—a rosette on her forehead, and three lines on her chin. Her full lips curved upward in an unrestrained smile, and her dark brown eyes glittered with vitality.

"I hope you'll tell me a little about your life," I said, as we settled down with Cokes in the lounge. An older woman had come with Maria—Tugli Obara was the name that, slowly and intently, she wrote in my notebook. Friend or relative? They didn't say.

"Do you have children?" I asked Maria, guessing that she was in her early twenties at the most.

"I have two children," she told me in a velvet voice. "They are two years and four years. I have a relative who takes care of them while I work at Ambua; I pay her a salary," she said, lifting her head proudly.

"I went to the Catholic Mission School through grade six," she went on, as though she'd been asked about education before. "Then I went to technical school. I learned about cooking, sewing, and family planning."

"What did they teach about family planning?"

"I learned it is not so good to have children too close together. So I learned which days it is all right for husband and wife to be together, and which days it is not all right."

In Huli lore, there were only four days when it was all right for husband and wife to "be together"—right at the middle of the monthly cycle. Yet in Catholic teaching, those are exactly the days not to be together sexually if family planning is a goal. But I didn't sense a way to find out how Maria resolved this contradiction, if, in fact she did.

"Do you and your husband share a house?" I inquired.

"We do," she said. She sat erect, intent on our conversation. Tugli stayed quiet, occasionally nodding to agree with something Maria said. "My grandparents live in separate houses, but my parents are Catholics and they live together like we do. But right now, my husband is working on a boat on the Sepik River."

"So you both earn cash. Who decides how it should be spent?"

"When my husband is away, I decide how to use the money I earn. When he is here, we decide together. But in most Huli families, the man controls how the money is spent." She paused, as though choosing her words carefully. "It is because of the bride-price—when that is paid, he has the right to control his wife. After the bride-price is paid, a wife cannot go back to her family, and some Huli men treat their wives badly, some beat them. It is only if he kills her, or if the wife hangs herself, that there must be compensation." Maria's voice was level and her face told me nothing. Tugli looked somber.

I sat silently, digesting this stunning news under the guise of sipping my drink. Maria's account was more shocking than that of anthropologist Stephen Frankel, who began working among the Hulis in 1977. Most wrongs could be righted through compensation, he wrote, although women whose bones were fractured by their husbands were often ashamed to demand it.

But then shame deters American women from revealing beatings inflicted by husbands or lovers—shame and an inner conviction that they deserved what they got. The shame is the woman's, not the man's. Among the Hulis, as Maria stated, the shame became the man's only if he killed the woman or caused her suicide. The shame became his because his kin were then forced to join in paying compensation to her kin.

"Huli women work much harder than men." Maria broke into the leaden silence. "Men build the houses and clear for the gardens, but women do the work in the gardens and take care of the children and the pigs." These were modern women, I surmised, since traditional men harvested their own crops and cared for their sons.

"As we see them walking on the road, with their *bilums* filled with huge loads, the women look very strong," I said. "Do women believe they are strong, Maria?"

"I don't know. But they think their life is very hard."

"What do the women think when they see travelers like us?" I wondered. "We must look very strange. Look at me, I'm wearing pants. Huli women don't wear pants."

"No," she said earnestly, "but they want to be like you, to dress like you. They see that husband and wife are together, and like to be together. Husband and wife show respect to each other."

"Yes, many husbands and wives do like and respect each other," I said. "My husband and I like each other *very* much. But it's sometimes different in the United States. About half our marriages end in divorce, and some of our women have hard lives too," I added, wondering if their glimpses of travelers were making highland women feel inferior.

Then I told the story of Janice, a young woman who helped me clean my house, just as Maria helped clean the lodge. Janice had two small children too, but she had no husband. She cleaned other people's homes for eight or nine hours every day. In return, she earned barely enough cash for food, for fuel to warm her thin-walled trailer during the long, frigid winter, and for gasoline for the aging car that took her to her jobs. She rarely had time to be with her children except when they were sick, and then she lost her pay. Janice did have a mother—her father was dead—and a sister who minded the children while Janice worked. But, I explained, there were women like Janice who lived far from their families; some lived completely alone.

Maria and Tugli shook their heads slowly, looking troubled, so I turned the conversation back to more familiar ground. "You told me you have two children," I said. "Did you give birth to them at home?"

"No, I had my babies at the Health Center," Maria explained. "Many women do that now, but they used to give birth in a special house in the bush. The woman would be alone; her mother and other women would bring food for her, but nobody would help her."

"Why not?" I asked in dismay.

"She wouldn't want others to see her like that. When it was time for the baby to come, they would tell her to work very hard in the garden, so she worked from early morning until late afternoon. They thought that would make the baby come easy.

"The woman stayed in the bush for four months and then came home. But for four more months the father could not see the baby. If he did, he must sacrifice a pig or else, if he was in a war and an arrow went into his body, the wound wouldn't heal."

"You mean, sacrifice a pig to a spirit that will protect him?" I asked, and both Maria and Tugli nodded.

"I understand that men fear the fluids that come from women's bodies in childbirth and also in the menstrual period," I told her.

"Do women feel that they have special power because of that—the power to harm men?"

Maria frowned and glanced at Tugli with a puzzled expression. After a pause, she shook her head. "I don't know. Men think it's something dirty coming from the body, and women think that too. But girls who go to school learn that it comes from the ovaries after the egg is ready."

"Is there any special celebration when a girl has her first menstrual period?" I asked, letting her misconception pass by.

"No," Maria said. "But then her mother teaches her how she must clean herself. She must not look at a man during that time. If she does, he must sacrifice a pig or else he might become sick."

"You say some women think it's dirty. Do they go to special houses?"

"It was the tradition that a woman would go into the bush during that time. Now she stays in one end of her house, and she must wash her body and hands often. She can cook food for herself and her daughters, but her sons must go to the father's house." I wondered what happened if mother and father were sharing a house in the Christian way, but decided to stay with Maria's perspective right now.

"I'm told that some boys are taken away from their mothers when they're very young," I said.

"Yes," Maria agreed. "When they are four, or maybe when they are three."

"Does the mother feel sad when her boy is taken away?" I asked—I would have felt wrenching pain if I had been separated from my son when he was three or four. But, once again, Maria looked bewildered, and shook her head in negation.

"No," she said calmly. "They do not feel sad because it is the custom." Tugli nodded her head in agreement. "It is the custom," she murmured.

◈ ◈ ◈

I was jolted by surprise when the women denied the sadness. Surprise and shock. But why? Except for the interludes of nursing, the care of Huli children seemed shared within the family group. Women here didn't corral their children and themselves in isolated homes, where resentment can grow like a noxious weed in the tangled garden of love.

How well my years as a psychotherapist had taught me that some women love their children and some don't, some want to but can't. My own mother was mired in dreams at first, and then in disappointments.

She once glided into my bedroom to say good night when I was three or four. It was usually nanny's job; that was *our* custom. Mother may have wanted to show herself as a princess on her way to a ball—a vision in sapphire blue lace sparkling with rhinestones. A mantilla framed her ivory face.

"Good night, darling," she said, eluding my upraised arms. "Don't muss my hair." Maybe she meant the "darling" then. It wasn't until after the laces, the diamonds, the balls, the fashionable villas and famous friends had all turned into pumpkins that I ceased to be a darling.

When my father began leaving the family, Mother couldn't bear not being alluring enough to hold him. When the separation was final, the insult to her self-esteem was too intense, and she began imagining that other people were to blame for her diminished life.

Gradually, insidiously, she spun her paranoid ideas around me. Why me? Because my older sister was gone and my younger sister was more compliant? Because I was becoming a rebellious teen who scorned the Social Register and all it stood for? I never knew why, but as her delusional web expanded she imagined me at the center of a widening plot against her. Her darling became a devil.

I couldn't free myself from that web; I couldn't free my mother until her terror was so intense that she agreed to enter a hospital "for a rest." But even after that ten-year nightmare began fading, my urge to free trapped people lingered on.

◈ ◈ ◈

So in the freshness of a highland morning, after a dawn excursion with Joseph Tano to see raggiana birds of paradise displaying plumage that glowed like the sunrise, we wandered toward town to visit the Tari District Women's Center. We might discover programs there that Pirip would want to know about.

Walking up a narrow lane, we passed women clustered inside one of the spiked Huli gates. "They're playing bingo," Joseph said derisively. "They play from six in the morning to six at night." Further along, women huddled at roadside playing cards, tossing out bets of kina notes, while men stood around watching.

We passed the central market, the airport, the police station and then came to a cluster of metal-roofed buildings shielded by a chain-link fence. *HAUS KAI* announced a sign on one structure, and women were cooking food, or *kaikai,* in a huge cauldron steaming over an outside hearth. A vegetable garden and guest house were protected by more fences. Outside the main building, a thin, auburn-haired woman with alabaster skin, a brown-skinned woman, and three men were sitting on the ground in a circle, intensely involved in discussion.

"Good morning," I said.

"Good morning," they chorused, looking up curiously.

"I can see that you're busy now, but I'd like to come back for a visit." I explained my interest, and the white-skinned woman smiled.

"I'm Robyn," she said. "I'm an Australian advisor to the women, and this is Jacinta. She's the president of the Tari District Women's Association." She deferred to the highlander with a gracious gesture. There was some swift discussion and we agreed on a day.

When Bob and I returned, we found Jacinta in a small office opening off the side of the main building, sitting behind a desk stacked high with file folders. A photo of Queen Elizabeth II hung on the wall above, and I suddenly understood why there was a plethora of Elizabeths and Bettys among highland women. I had supposed it was a biblical Elizabeth whose name had been bestowed in Christian baptisms, but here was a more likely figure, the head of the British Commonwealth. Papua New Guinea was a member.

Now Robyn joined us, looking quizzically at Bob—he hadn't come into the center before. I introduced him as a doctor interested in women's health, and she nodded her acceptance.

Jacinta was a full-figured woman with broad features and cropped hair, who was coughing and sneezing explosively today. "I think I am getting some kind of influenza," she explained, wiping her streaming eyes and nose on the hem of her cotton skirt. With no immunity against the viruses of PNG, I was torn between wanting to distance myself—impossible in this small space—and wanting to lean forward in conversation. I tried to slide my hand inconspicuously over my nose each time the droplets sprayed out.

"So you are the president," I ventured.

"That is true," said Jacinta, smiling slightly. "I was the founder and now I am the acting president. The district association includes ninety groups."

"That large?" I was surprised, but Robyn explained that Tari Basin was much larger than Wahgi Valley—it was about the size of the entire Western Highlands Province.

"How did you happen to start the association?"

"I started this work in 1983 because I believed that women needed help. Many women are deserted by their husbands when their husbands take a second wife, usually a younger wife," Jacinta said with a scornful quirk of her mouth. "Then women cannot take care of themselves and their children. Sometimes they can return to their own families, but not always."

"I'm confused," I told her. "When we first came, we were told that Huli women are independent, growing food in their own gardens and raising their children in their own houses—and that Huli men keep wives in different parts of the valley. And here's what I understood from an anthropologist who lived here in the 1950s."

Robert Glasse had written that only certain rights were acquired by a man through bride-price, and certain duties were acquired as well. A bridegroom had the right to decide where the bride would live, and the duty to build her a house. He had exclusive sexual rights, and the duty to make the proper magical preparations before intercourse. He had the right of fatherhood to children born in the marriage, and the right to have his wife join in raising the children and tending the gardens and pigs.

But he had no right to expect his wife to perform domestic services for him. She would not harvest his crops, prepare and cook his food, or work in the men's house.

Furthermore, Huli women had significant rights themselves. A woman could initiate a marriage, thus gaining the right to a sexual relationship with her husband, even if it wasn't an exclusive one. She could initiate a separation and could not be forced to return to her husband if she left him. She had some influence over the distribution of her bride-price. She could own pigs and other valuables, and give them away if she chose.

"Those were the traditions," Robyn agreed, "but they've been changing fast. The Christian churches urge men to have only one wife at a time."

"When I started this work, I thought it did not help the women to come telling their stories and crying," Jacinta broke in. "I wanted to help them become self-reliant. They had to find ways to earn cash using their own skills so they could take care of themselves. I encouraged them to grow crops for market, to learn to use sewing machines to make clothing, to raise chickens. And they run the *haus kai* here."

"How have men responded? For example, is violence against women a problem now?" I asked, thinking of Maria's stories.

"It is a big problem," Jacinta said. "Robyn works with that. Rape is common. Here is an example." She paused to daub at her dripping nose. "I know a girl who was called out of her family house by a man she knew, then he tried to rape her. Her family came out to help. They told the man he would have to marry the girl since nobody else would marry her now, and he would have to pay bride-price.

"A fine thing that is, to have to marry your raper," Robyn said caustically. "The family wouldn't even take her to hospital to find out if the man had actually entered her. Eighty percent of rapes are by someone the woman knows; I gave a seminar about it in

Moresby. The men were horrified, some of them were even in tears when they heard the figures."

"I do not know how it is that men can do such things," Jacinta chimed in. "We are their sisters, their mothers. We give birth to them, we feed them when they are so little, so soft." Her eyes filled with fresh tears, but these weren't caused by a virus. "How can they forget? When they beat women or rape women, how would they feel if it was their own sister or mother?"

The four of us sat silently, weighted by sadness.

"I've been wondering, now that younger men and women are living in the same house, are problems of violence increasing?" I asked after a few minutes.

"Yes they are," said Jacinta, and Robyn broke in heatedly, "Things are going *backward* for women with the rapid development. The Hulis were always a violent people, but it used to be channeled. Now it's broken loose, it goes everywhere, it's out of control and often turned against women and children. When a boy sees violence in his own family, he becomes that way too. We have little boys beating little girls."

"It's not only the Hulis," I said, describing a newspaper story of two seven-year-old boys who tried to rape a six-year-old girl in California. "It's said that four million women in my country were battered or killed by husbands or lovers in a recent year—that's more than the whole population of PNG. And almost a quarter of females in my country may be raped in their lifetime. I'm ashamed to tell you that, but we are doing things about it." I told them about Hot Lines and Safe Houses, and I explained how they worked. "Do you have shelters for women who are raped or beaten?"

"No, if we tried to shelter women, men would come and attack us both with axes," Robyn answered, and I heard Bob stifle a groan.

"Do the police give any protection? We noticed the station right next door."

"No," she said bitterly, twisting in her chair. "The police themselves are involved in rape, sometimes gang rape! We don't even get much help through the local court, and no support from the provincial or national government. And there's no sympathy for women who work for women. Jacinta's husband left her, and I had a high-lander boyfriend, but that ended because of my work."

"I'm sorry to hear that," I sympathized, intensely aware of Bob. But this was no time to mention his encouragement—it might have seemed boastful—so I told them about Pirip, and the help Kuru gave to her efforts.

"There must be only a handful like that in PNG," Robyn lamented, and Jacinta nodded, daubing her nose again. Just then, a man came to the door with a question for Robyn and Jacinta and, with apologies, they went out.

I was glad for the intermission because questions were buzzing through my mind. I wondered again whether Kuru's nights in the men's house, where his masculinity was buttressed, helped him feel secure in encouraging Pirip's efforts to promote change among women. Yet change among women meant change for men, and I was curious about other motives for Kuru's involvement. Pirip had told me nothing yet about her private relationship with her husband—maybe that story held the key.

Just then, Robyn's discouraged voice broke into my thoughts as she and Jacinta came back. "There is so much work to be done, including paper work. We needed help, so it was Jacinta's idea to apply for two Peace Corps volunteers from America. We have a married couple—they've been here a week."

"I hope they can visit some of the women's groups throughout the valley," Jacinta explained.

"Do you get any financial support from the government?" I asked.

"No. The Women's Center is a non-governmental organiza-tion—an NGO. Provincial funds do not reach rural women." Jacinta said, confirming what Pirip had told me.

"But we do have literacy workers here," Robyn added. "That is a major government push."

"How did you get involved in this work, Robyn?" Bob asked—he'd been an unobtrusive listener.

"I've been a feminist for years," she said. "I started law school, then I decided to become a paralegal instead. I've worked with abo-riginal women in Australia, and PNG women for the past five years.

Above A view of the Wahgi Valley shows the Wahgi River, the Trans-Niugini Highway, and *pitpit* in the foreground.

A Kuma woman places *kaukau* and other tubers on banana leaves in preparation of a *mumu*.

Above A mother leads her children home with her bilums bulging and a stalk of bananas balanced on her head.

Left Traditional Kuma women planting *kaukau* with digging sticks in a new garden.

Pirip, her family, and members of the women's association gather together to welcome the author and her husband.

Pirip's *Haus Win,* the "centerpiece" of her center for women.

From the mission where Pirip lived in her childhood, she points toward her birthplace in the distant mountains.

Pirip stands in front of her new trade store. Its traditional woven walls rest on a modern cement foundation and support a corrugated metal roof.

uru, Pirip's husband, secures a young banana ee in their garden.

A Kuma woman in traditional festive attire faces one dressed as missionaries have decreed.

Left A Huli warrior demonstrates his skill with bow and arrows.

Above A Huli elder sports a ceremonial wig.

Left The author crosses a traditional bridge in the forest near Ambua Lodge.

A Huli mother and her daughters dressed in ceremonial attire. Her son stands with them in front of the women's house.

Women with laden bilums at the Tari market which also serves as a social center.

The Karawari River reflects a woman fishing as her husband gently poles their dugout canoe close to the shore.

Right Hidden from the missionaries, Pokiambut, an ancient totem, gives power to the people of Chimbut Village.

Below, left In traditional attire and decoration, a mother greets visitors at Yimas Two.

Below, right A woman in Yimas Two performs a dance of welcome.

With its live-aboard family, a floating market makes its way slowly down the Arafundi River.

A little fisherman skillfully balances in his own dugout canoe.

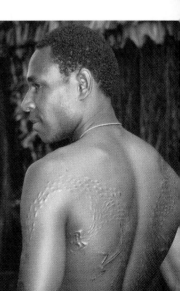

Facial decoration is a highly developed art form among Arafundi River people.

Far right A Sepik River youth proudly displays scars from initiation rites.

A woman rinses the woven strainers used in the preparation of sago flour.

A woman ladles water over a strainer basket of sago pulp as she prepares flour for gruel and pancakes.

A Karawari woman prepares a meal of sago gruel and greens as another woman weaves a straw mat in the background.

But I think I'll be going back to Australia in about six months; I'm really quite worn out. I'd like to go to a beach again and, well, I'd like to be able to wear a bathing suit safely again, too." For a moment, she looked wistful and very young.

When I turned to Jacinta to say good-bye, I saw bewilderment in her eyes. Was she puzzled about Robyn's longings? Or was she thinking of those little, soft, baby boys cradled at her breasts, and wondering how their maleness had gone awry?

◈ ◈ ◈

Jacinta's bewilderment and Robyn's exhaustion were easy to understand; I felt wrenched and weary myself. We had come back to PNG in recoil from the rising violence in our own nation, only to find storms of aggression raging through the highlands—and much of it was directed against women. I needed a retreat, a time-out to gain fresh perspective, before I made contact with Pirip again. Fortunately, Bob and I had planned an immersion in the calming rhythms of the lowland rain forests, and we'd be flying there the next day.

Chapter Eleven

MAGICAL RIVERS

W ill you fly visually?" I asked the pilot when we boarded a small plane at Tari. Great billows of cumulus clouds obscured the surrounding peaks and we were to cross the spine of PNG—the Central Range that thrusts its summits over 12,000 feet in the air.

"No," said the sunburned, sandy-haired man. "We do that a lot, but I have satellite navigation here," and he gestured toward the instrument panel. "We put it in last year." Just before the race toward takeoff, he glanced back. "I'll be flying over the Porgera mine," he said. "If we're lucky, we'll see it on the starboard side."

Lucky? Tailings from the gold mine had been dumped into the river that coursed through the mountains, across the Papuan Plateau, and then along the coastal flats, carrying a poisonous residue to the reefs and creatures of the gulf. It wasn't Porgera I wanted to see.

I was tempted to refuse to look. But I did—with the same compulsion that pulls my eyes toward an accident on the highway. Grudgingly, I looked down to a wound in the mountainside below, oozing its yellow-brown pus into water that once was pure.

Then it was gone from view. As the clouds swirled apart, the landscape looked as though a giant hand had seized a bolt of dark green velvet and creased it into a multitude of pleats. A river coiled among them like a silver snake. Then we were beyond the mountains, whose turbulent air currents caused the clouds to gather, and the view opened onto a sodden lowland where rivers had broadened into lakes, and lakes had flooded through the forest—greens melded with blues that reflected the sky. The rains were heavy this year

We swooped lower and the illusion of velvet was gone. Now the ground seemed densely packed with broccoli heads, some thrusting high toward the sun. We saw a straggle of bush huts along a ridge above the Karawari River (a major tributary that flowed north to join the distant Sepik), and they were centered by a building whose roof soared to a peak at each end in the style of a *haus tambaran,* a spirit house. This cluster was not only a village; it was the familiar shelter of Karawari Lodge.

Our landing nearby was smooth, and the Kiwi pilot flushed at our praise. Nine years before, our first landing here was feather light. "Would it be satisfactory to fly to Karawari in a helicopter?" Bob Bates asked us when our plane failed to pick us up in Mt. Hagen. Quite satisfactory, we said. Would it ever! How could anyone refuse the chance to float through the heavens in a *Mixmaster Bilong Jesus Christ,* the enchanting pidgin name?

Back for the third time now, we boarded a stubby, flat-bottomed craft powered by an outboard motor to travel from the airstrip to the landing below the lodge. Relishing every instant of our return, we declined a ride in a well-worn van and walked up the steep, red clay track. Slipping, our thongs sucked off by tenacious ooze, and gazed at in wonder by local people resting in the shade of their pandanus dwellings, we arrived at the main lodge building drenched in sweat. A slender, stately woman named Lena greeted us, holding out a basket of towels.

As we savored cool moist cloth against hot moist skin, I scanned the dim recesses behind Lena—the soaring of the high thatched roof, the great wooden columns of support, the huge and intricate carvings that men from faraway Sepik villages had sent upriver for display. My eyes searched the cross-beams until an image came into focus.

After a day of exploration in 1983, Bob and I, a visiting entomologist, and the homesick Australian couple who managed the lodge had gathered before the evening meal, lazing back in our chairs, unfocused gazes sweeping the upper reaches, when a flicker of motion caught our attention. Stretched along the highest beam, an eight-foot python was joining in our tranquillity. It posed no threat to us at all, but the opposite wasn't true. There was an urgent shout, and a man came running to hurl a spear with lethal accuracy and bring the creature down. A tactical mistake, the python had made—in joining us at a meal, it became a meal instead.

Simeon, the new manager, greeted us now in an aura of amiable agitation that swirled around the edges of Lena's pool of calm. "Do you have a wonderful view for us, Simeon?" I asked, and he escorted us to bungalow number five, whose small verandah overlooked an oceanic expanse of rain forest bounded only at the northwestern horizon by blue mountain ridges. He assured himself that the ceiling fan worked (while the generator ran), and the mosquito netting was properly draped, and then he slipped away. We stood bewitched. Gazing across this wilderness that teems with myriad unseen forms of life engaged in their intricate work of birthing, feeding, mating, dying, we felt connected with the elemental rhythms of the earth.

But our biologies were still trained to the clock, so we followed a deep-throated drumbeat to the source of some midday food. In the huge gathering room we met a tall, slim, muscular man with burnished dark skin. He was Paul Api, our guide. "What would you like to see?" he asked.

"The last time we came here, the villagers put on some *sing-sings*," I explained. "Now we'd like to learn about the everyday lives of your people, and the ways you turn to the rain forest for your needs."

I didn't voice the rest. Were the river people caught in the surge that was propelling Pirip and cresting across Tari Basin? And since surges are two-way currents, was it pulling women backward or forward? And what about the men?

◈ ◈ ◈

After our meal, we started up the roiling, clay-colored river. To elude the strongest currents, Paul steered to the far bank where silvery plumes of *pitpit* leaned over the glistening water, as though admiring their own reflections. As each arching blade of foliage touched the calmer water here, its reflection completed a faultless ellipse. Within the camouflage of the many ellipses, two elegant pied herons were standing, their ebony bodies crowned with snow-white heads.

"The people use them as crocodile bait," Paul told us and I

winced. "We also use the feathers to decorate ourselves for our *singsings.*"

Behind the *pitpit*, the jungle struggled toward the sun, weighed down by tangles of vines seeking light of their own. Densely cloaked trees that had broken under their burden sagged like weary primordial giants, yet *galubia* palms soared above the canopy, sometimes to ninety feet.

"The ladies shred those leaves to make skirts and fans," said Paul. "The shoots of the *galubia* are yellow inside, and we use that color for body decoration when we have a *singsing.*"

The greenery was punctuated here and there by an orange-red blaze of lupinelike blossoms cascading down the trees, sometimes in twenty-foot lengths of vine or more. "Some call that Flame of the Forest. The stems hold water for drinking," Paul explained. "And the ladies can use that water to prevent starting a baby." We were motoring slowly past a living pharmacy. There was the *gipma* whose warmed leaves were used to ease pain, the young *endin* tree whose stems held liquid that calmed diarrhea, the ginger whose leaves were brewed to treat malaria, and whose blossoms were nourishing too.

"Could there be a cure for AIDS growing in there?"I asked Bob.

"Sure there could. Question is, will the ethnobotanists get here first or the loggers?" New Guinea forests were amazingly diverse; among 9,000 species of trees and plants on this island, eighty percent were found nowhere else in the world. Yet they were being ravaged by Asian timber companies in collusion with avaricious politicians.

Yimas Two, Paul's village, was our destination for the afternoon. His people, the Tamblakmeri, moved downstream from Yimas One in the 1930s and settled at the juncture of two rivers. Today, the waters of the Arafundi were racing down from their mountain headwaters where rains had been torrential; they were forming huge whirlpools as they joined the Karawari.

Our outboard propelled us steadily through this turmoil. But as we approached the village, we were startled to see a small nude boy balanced on a floating thirty-foot log, his toes grasping the wet bark like suction cups as he guided his shifting support with a pole. A man—perhaps the father—paddled a dugout canoe nearby, but there was no physical linkage between man and child, nor between boat and log. Not many yards away, another solitary lad—about four years old, Paul guessed—moved nimbly in a narrow, tippy canoe, tying a blue fishing line to the carved crocodile's head that formed the prow.

I thought back to the year our agile son was four. Would we have allowed him alone in a canoe on a turbulent river? No, nor on a calm river either. Engrossed with his carefully chosen toys, did he feel the competence these two boys displayed in their movements? Quite doubtful. Did he feel himself a valued actor in the work of our household, like the boy who was bringing home a needed log? Unlikely.

Here, floodwater was a time of bounty. The currents offered a harvest of uprooted trees for house building and boat making while sturdy house-poles, sunk six feet deep in the river bed, held the stilted dwellings of Yimas Two against the surge. The waters were so high that villagers could step directly from their canoes to the floors of their homes.

Paul bumped the bow of our craft into the muddy bank, and we scrambled out where several women had gathered to greet us. In this village, said Paul, the women wove mats and made grass skirts that they traded upriver for sago starch. Today they were wearing traditional attire, prepared for a ceremonial dance of welcome.

The beauty of one young woman was riveting. Her shredded palm skirt, dyed amber, russet, and black, encircled her pelvis below the brown, taut roundness of her pregnant belly. Her pendant breasts, with huge brown-black areolas and prominent nipples, were so full that we inferred she still nursed the child—two or three years old—who snuggled against her left shoulder. An elaborate white design began at her forehead, curled around her glistening eyes, crossed her cheek bones, accented her flaring nostrils, and continued around her smiling mouth. Above her high forehead, strands of her frizzy black hair had been intertwined to form two projections like the antennae of a butterfly.

The dancing ground was flooded, and she led us to a higher space where her companions waited, adorned with coronas of scarlet hibiscus and white frangipani. They wore grass skirts, and had tied shredded foliage to their arms and to the wands they waved. As the rhythm sped up, they circled, dipping their fluid knees and stamping their feet until a tiny tornado seemed to swirl through the village.

Now the sun was low so we started downriver to the lodge. With the outboard shut off, we floated in silence as hornbills and parrots-in-pairs flew above us, seeking their shelter for the night.

Our own comfortable shelter was shared with a plethora of insects. Net curtains hung across the windows, but our light attracted bugs through the sago palm roof. The netting around the beds could not deter the smallest and meanest, so we put our light out early.

We lay in a tiny island in an oceanic jungle. Even after the forest creatures had quieted in the waning light, even after the blackness in our cabin was absolute, I sensed an elemental throb in rhythm with my heart.

◈　◈　◈

We woke at first light to a swelling chorus of rain-forest birds. Until the hum of the generator intruded, we were held in thrall by the squawks, the chirps, the whistles, the trills that greeted the rising sun.

And then a bass voice joined the chorus. BOOM. BOOM. Boom, boom, boom. It was the resonant tone of the *garamut* drum, a hollowed-out span of the *garamut* tree with a slit along its length. BOYS. GIRLS. Come to school. It summoned the children asleep in riverside dwellings for miles around. Wake-up call was at seven—a reminder at seven-thirty. The signal of school starting came at eight, then children were singing their national anthem at the primary school below.

Paul eased our craft upriver again, careful not to create a wave that would swamp the fishing boats hugging the shore to avoid the current. Each was a long, narrow dugout canoe, scarcely wide enough for the slim bodies of the paddlers. The prows, rising above the waterline, had been carved into the ferocious shape of a crocodile's head. In many of the boats, blue smoke rose from embers smoldering in a pottery hearth traded upriver from the distant Chambri lakes—a shallow bowl with one side higher than the other, contoured into graceful scallops.

"I'm surprised that fire is needed in this heat," Bob said to Paul.

"It is to keep the mosquitoes away," Paul explained. "And it is to light cigarettes that our people make from local tobacco. And it is to cook some of the fishes when they are hungry."

In some canoes, a sheet of *limbom* palm bark had been curved into a shelter from sun and rain, and we saw young faces peeking out. "We use the *limbom* bark for water containers too, and to make a tray for sago pancakes," said Paul.

"I notice that it's mostly women who are out fishing," I remarked.

"We have a story about that," he told me. "It is The Legend of the Cormorant."

> Long ago, a woman set her fishing trap. No fish came, but she caught a cormorant. She was going to kill him, but he begged her not to, and said he would teach her his fishing skills. So she let him go, and that night he came to her in a dream and told her his secrets. And that is how women came to be good fishers.

As we glided along, a fishtail palm caught my eye. Its foliage supposedly looked like the forked tail of a fish, but to my eyes, it spread in the form of two huge wings.

"The inside part of this palm is soft and powerful," Paul told us. "If you throw the inside into the river, it makes the water spirits powerful and it makes the river wide. If you throw it into the lakes, the crocodiles will float and people can catch them. If a child dies, the mother or father will cut off the joint of one finger, and drill a hole in the palm, and push the finger into the soft inner part of the palm. This will give special power to the spirit in the palm, which will go to the family of the one who caused the child's death and cause a *payback*."

There was another palm that swooped fifty feet upward and outward, sheltering the villages beneath it.

"This is our tree of life," Paul said quietly. And as we turned up the Arafundi, close to Yimas Two, we saw one reason why this was so. A long palm had been hauled up on the bank, and people were clustered around it.

"They are preparing sago," Paul explained. This one tree, maybe fourteen years of age, felled before its starch became concentrated in its single enormous fruit, would feed five or six families for three weeks—if the right taboos had been observed. The name of the fish-tail palm musn't be mentioned in the presence of sago, or the sago wouldn't produce.

Paul steered into shore so we could watch. With strong blows from steel axes, two men ruptured the bark. Then women moved forward with long, sharp poles, to pry open the split and expose the fibrous pith inside. As they strained and pulled, they talked and laughed and slid into the river for cooling dips.

Other women moved forward with wooden tools that were both pick and mallet, sharp on one side and blunt on the other, to pound the pulp and separate its fibers. The pulp would be heaped into a trough, and water would be ladled over it to loosen the starch and carry it on through a woven fiber sieve. Finally, all of the starch would settle under a pool of rust-red water in the waiting recepta-cle—a canoe. That sociable work, with more talk and laughter and dips in the river, would occupy a day.

Later, we saw the pinkish-white starch being prepared for a meal. One woman squatted before a clay cauldron stirring a gruel of sago and water, with a basket of greens nearby to enrich the gluey stew. Another crouched over a clay skillet in which a large sago pan-cake slowly baked. When we tasted an offered morsel, it had a dry, chewy texture but no flavor at all.

"We make salt from the sago bark," Paul told us. "The young bark is cut out, you dry it in the sun, you burn it on the fire, and you collect the ashes. You put them through a container like a coconut shell with holes. Then you mix them with water and strain it into another container." But there was no salt here now.

The women at Yimas Two were working in worn T-shirts and cotton skirts today. As one of them squatted, I saw cut-off trousers

underneath her skirt. It was a hot and bulky combination, but exposure of her vulva would disgrace her and insult the men who might
see. The grasses of a traditional skirt would have fallen gracefully
between her legs.

"Slow down," I wanted to say. "Let me tell you about my highland friend, Pirip. Some think that women are losing advantages as
they take on Western ways." I didn't say it—it was too complex a
story and Paul was nudging us to move on.

Paul's formal schooling was brief but, like Joseph in Ambua, he
looked, listened, and smelled the river and the forest and had realms
of knowledge that we would never share. And he was an eager
teacher.

"These are called *gumba* trees," he said as we passed a sweep
of heart-shaped leaves and long panacles of delicate pink blossoms.
"People believe this tree makes rain. They take the bark and put it
into water. When it rots, the rain will come. And the women use the
fibers of this tree to weave *bilums* too."

The tall, straight *erima* tree and the *sanda* tree were used for
dugouts. And the *sanda,* with its large, serrated oval leaves, yielded
oil for the skin and hair. Paul pointed to the *endin* tree, whose long,
narrow leaves were used to treat malaria, and the *ton* tree that
yielded nuts and timber.

He showed us pandanus, whose leaves were woven into hats,
and pointed toward two towering hardwoods—*kwila,* used for
houseposts, and *garamut,* used for long, richly carved drums for ceremony and signal. He pulled close to the plum shrub with fernlike
leaves whose juices were squeezed onto ringworm. He showed us
the breadfruit, with its glossy, large-lobed leaves and edible fruit,
and the *kumbian* tree in whose big leaves certain foods were
wrapped for baking.

"When ladies have sex and are just becoming pregnant, they can
cut the *kumbian* tree, and, as the water leaks out, the baby will be
released. Or they can cut the roots of breadfruit trees, and the lady
will be released from the baby." Did that belief stimulate uterine
contractions? Or are there chemicals in the sap of those trees that do
the same thing? Those were unspoken questions as I remembered

my first meeting with Pirip's companion, Betty Kaman, who seemed to have forgotten the control over their reproduction that women traditionally exercised.

In the dry season, said Paul, cane was used as a source of water. "But if your wife is pregnant," he warned, "a man must not cut the cane for water because that might cause his wife to release the baby. He must search for a stream or a waterfall. And when a wife is having a baby, the man should wear a *laplap* or else she'll get a lot of pain."

Now a birdcall rang across the silence. "A tree pigeon," Paul said, but we didn't really believe him. It sounded to us like a magic flute. We were floating on a magical river where human needs for food, shelter, warmth, light, utensils, adornment, music, weapons, transportation, medicine, and for spiritual power were met in the dense greenery around us.

◈ ◈ ◈

Paul took us upriver to Yimas One, rising steeply from the lapping water. We sheltered from pelting rain in the airy interior of a family house. The flooring of springy *limbom* palm was immaculately clean, and we saw Chambri clay hearths for cooking, and mosquito nets for sleeping—modern netting traded downriver, not the palm mosquito bags that women traditionally wove.

Marriages were usually arranged, Paul explained when I asked. The exchange of a female cousin for another man's cousin—still common—was the traditional source of wives. Bride-price was not expected; something else used to happen.

"A boy would have to go through his initiation, and then he was sent on a head-hunting raid. He would cut off a person's head and pour the blood over a special stone, and then he would eat the flesh. And then the boy and the girl who would be his wife can come together." I was glad he hadn't told us during our picnic lunch.

As we motored downriver, threading our way through tangles of torn branches and weeds, we came to a floating market being guided in the current. Huge logs had been lashed together with vines, forming a platform that was piled with sheaves of sago roofing. Mammoth stalks of bananas had been heaped on top of that.

On the back half of the platform there was a shelter, dimly lighted by a glowing fire. A small boy stood at the entrance, frowning as we approached, while two bare-breasted women nursing their babies turned, their eyes flashing white, their mouths curving into friendly smiles.

Manpower served as the engine: A grinning youth in blue shorts poled at the stern, and several men paddled dugout canoes that were piled with more bananas and lashed to the raft.

"Please, let's go slowly," I said to Paul, so we quieted our motor and drifted nearby. As the river carried this edifice, it carried a family within their home; it carried their home within their workplace—this market that they floated from village to village, bartering for needed supplies.

River life wasn't riddled with the isolating splits that development imposes—splits between home and office, work and play, parent and child. Splits were zigzagging through the highlands: Betty Kaman used Australian nursing bottles to free her from child-care for teaching; Maria paid a babysitter while she cleaned Ambua lodge.

I had been split when my daughter was born. Breast feeding was finding favor again after three decades of bottles-on-schedule. I liked the new yet old way. I liked having a thin stream of milk spurt from my taut nipple into the searching mouth; I liked the fuzz of my daughter's head nestling into my armpit; I liked my breasts, swollen like Marilyn Monroe's.

But breasts were for the bedroom; they shouldn't leave the house unless they were disciplined in a stiff, pointed bra. And even with discreet drop-down panels, nursing was for the home. I liked my nourishing, sensuous self. But I liked my curious, intellectual self too, and that self had to leave the house to do the work she was trained to do. So, like Betty Kaman, I bought bottles. I separated my selves and each one longed for the other.

Some in New England are trying to cobble split lives together again, reclaiming the past that Betty, Maria, and Pirip are pushing away—the past still present in the floating market. Some farming families school their young in their living rooms and turn the work of the field into a game. Some investment advisers carry on electronic conversations with clients from their homes while children dash in and out. Some editors . . .

"Take care!" Paul's warning broke into my musings; a contorted branch was about to jab me. But that night I dreamed of a floating market equipped with a solar-powered computer and a modem and fax.

◈ ◈ ◈

"Could you take us directly into the forest?" we asked Paul one day. "Yes," he said, "I know a place near Yimas Two." That afternoon he turned off-river and eased the boat into the primeval tangle. Yet it felt like a crashing intrusion so we asked him to silence the motor and we glided, steering with paddle and outstretched arms. We glided in tannin-rich mahogany water that mirrored every golden ginger blossom, every buttress root steadying the giant trees, every vine twining toward the sun.

So true were the reflections that we seemed suspended in a double world, discerning no line between water and air. The aerial roots of a strangler fig reached toward us and, as we craned skyward to see the monarch of the forest, this seemed like a holy place.

"The spirits in this tree are powerful," Paul told us. "When a woman is pregnant, she should not go close or the spirit will turn her baby upside down. Women cannot go into the bush alone— there must be five together.

"A man says, 'Spirit of tree, I'm going hunting, make my eyes clear.' The spirits can teach him how to hunt. The spirits teach witch doctors, they give power to young people. They have power to turn a man into a flying fox.

"Women spirits go after men at night. The tree-spirit woman from the strangler fig can lure a man into the forest to have sex. The man can go deaf, his eyes can go blind. He can disappear into the forest."

In this place of contorted shapes, eerie reflections, ambiguous realities, the possibility of disappearing forever seemed convincing. We turned back before the light could fail. But as we emerged from the deep silence of the creek, it seemed that we'd already been seized by a spirit of the strangler fig. Incredibly, there was rock music in the air.

"Is that a radio we're hearing?" Bob asked Paul.

"No, it is the disco at Yimas Two."

"The *what?*"

"Some boys are playing at Yimas Two."

"Can we go and see?" So Paul crossed the river again.

One end of a building, a men's rest house, had been roughly partitioned, and the musicians crouched in a small, dark, hot space—two guitarists, and a drummer. It wasn't the richly toned *garamut* nor the *kundu* drum that he played. He found his complex beat on a simulated electronic drum composed of a cardboard carton, a bundle of reeds, and two scraps of flattened metal. While we'd been enthralled with the voices of the past, these men had been reaching for the voices of their future. We recorded the music, and when we played it back, the drummer said gravely, "We thank you for your interest in the rock group of Yimas Two."

"Where have they heard rock music?" Bob asked as we floated toward the lodge. "Is there a short-wave radio in Yimas?"

"No," Paul said. "Maybe they have gone to Wewak [a northern coastal town]. Or they have heard one of the rock bands that toured out of Wewak, carrying its own generator." Paul was disgusted by rock, he told us, especially all the sexy vocals.

"I sing gospel music," he said, and later he let Bob tape his songs.

◈ ◈ ◈

One night I sweated through an interlude of fear, wakened by distant shouts that sounded like drunken revelry. In the black velvet stillness, when the pulse of the jungle had slowed, this was an ugly intrusion. It sounded like men out of control, breaking through constraining taboos.

"Are you awake?" I whispered to Bob and he was. He was calm when I voiced my dread, remembering tales we'd recently heard about Western-style violence in PNG, video violence, random violence. Had this come here with the rock groups from Wewak?

"Bob, do you realize we're in the middle of a jungle, without radio contact? Even if the generator was on, who would be listening now?" But he'd drifted back to sleep, so I lay in my shroud of netting and imagined ways to become invisible if there should be a raid on the lodge.

When Paul came in the morning, he was puzzled about my fear. Some boisterous young men called out and my imagination ran amok? As he steered the boat away from the landing, he steered my mind back to the traditions of his people. "If some spirits come to me at night and I cannot sleep, I take bark from some trees and burn it. The smell makes the spirits stay away."

"I will tell you about poisoning in Papua New Guinea," he went on—not a soothing subject, but unthreatening to me. "If I have a problem with a man, I will collect his spit, or cut one part of his shirt or pants. I'll give it to the poison man, and he'll put poison on it. He is very powerful. In three months, my enemy will die. If his family suspects what is happening, they can go to a witch doctor, pay a fee, and get the spell lifted. Or they can approach the poisoner and compensate him so he will lift the spell."

"In the highlands, we learned that people go to witch doctors when they're injured or sick. Is that true among your people, too?" Bob asked.

"It is," Paul said. "Many people go to witch doctors when they're sick, even Christians. I am a Christian. First I pray to God, but if I do not get well, I go to the witch doctor."

We'd been motoring down the Karawari, but now we turned up another tributary, the Konmei river. We pushed through strong currents again, and Paul steered toward the calmer shallows. We heard a deep, pulsing swoosh, and a hornbill flew over.

"I will tell you the Legend of the Hornbill." Paul said.

There was once a hunter who went hunting, and while hunting he saw hornbills sitting on a tree. He was trying to shoot one, but one hornbill said, "Let us live—this forest, it is ours." So the man went back home. The next day he went back to the same place without his bow and arrow to study the hornbill's secrets. The hornbills flew down to the ground, and then they changed into women, and they were bathing in a small stream. The man saw how the hornbill stripped off its skin and became human. It was very beautiful. He was trying to catch one to have as his wife.

So the man, he did. He took one hornbill skin home, then he came back and appeared to them. They got their skins and changed back, but one lady was left without a skin. So the man went near the lady and said, "Come to my home and you will be my wife." So the woman went with the man. They lived together, and the wife bore a son.

One day, the son was hungry, so his father went hunting. His wife stayed in the house, trying to find her hornbill skin. She found that the skin was on a frame for smoking skins and fresh meats. She put the skin into water to make it fresh, then tried to go inside it. She tried to fly, and she did. Then she put the skin back in a secret place.

When her husband came home, he looked around to see if the skin was still there. He found nothing, so he started to argue with his wife and fight with her. Night came, and when the man was asleep the lady got her skin and flew away. She did not come back.

This was a story of the hornbill clan, which included the people of Yimas; they were forbidden to kill hornbills or eat them. Many villages had a similar legend about the cassowary or cuckabarra, Paul told us (and, I later learned, that legend about women reclaiming their power was found in cultures outside of New Guinea too).

Lost in a mythic world, I'd stopped noticing our natural surround. A slashing torrent of rain brought me back abruptly, and Paul swung our boat toward a small marshy inlet. We were not the first ones there.

"It is a camp where a family may come for two or three weeks to fish and to smoke their fish," said Paul. A platform of *limbom* palm flooring had been erected on stilts, with an overhanging sago roof. In the dimness, veiled by blue smoke from two clay hearths, we discerned nine shapes.

Nine people, and I expected to see them huddled in chill, damp, silent misery. But they were talking cheerfully and, as we approached, the nearest woman turned with a dimpling smile. We sheltered near them, exchanging smiles and gestures and phrases of pidgin while they munched pandanus nuts—chewed when there was no betel at hand.

An older boy slid into his canoe and paddled through drowned plants to our stern. Gravely, he presented to Paul three fresh catfish wrapped in banana leaves. Bob and I supposed that they were being offered for sale, but we were wrong again. Paul's response was warm and effusive. "Gutpela, gutpela" (kind, good), he said in his resonant bass voice. The fish were a gift from the family's catch.

Chapter Twelve

SPIRITS OLD AND NEW

The air was filled with haunting music, plaintive dialogues of tone answering tone. In the spirit house of Chimbut, far up the Karawari River, men were playing the sacred flutes.

In mythic times, men stole the flutes from the women who first possessed them. Since then, these intricately carved instruments, up to three inches in diameter and in varying lengths, have played an essential and secret role in male rites.

"They are always played in pairs," Paul said as we walked into the remnants of a spirit house—*haus tambaran.* "Two flutes represent water spirits, two represent spirits of the cave, and the spirits meet in the playing. The longer flutes are female—they set the tune—and the shorter male flutes, they end it."

The men, their eyes dancing, drew the flutes across their mouths, holding the index finger of each hand over their lower lip and next to the hole in the flute. As one in a pair of players inhaled, the other blew; they varied their timing, their lipping, and their muting, creating eerie tones—no wonder women once believed them to be the voices of ancestor spirits. Or said they did, at least. But women were sitting among these men now.

"I thought the flutes were a closely guarded secret among men," I told Paul. "I'm told that in some highland clans a woman who saw the flutes could be put to death."

"Here, women could hear the flutes," Paul said, "but they must turn their backs. Boys could play them after the age of initiation, maybe fifteen," he added.

"Are initiation rites still practiced?" Bob asked.

"Not in this region, although some say that the custom is beginning again in Sepik villages," Paul said, his face inscrutable. These men, one with a toddler perched on his shoulders, were practicing for a competition in Wewak sponsored by a political party. This was election year and voters were being wooed.

"Chimbut is the main village of the *wantok* people," Paul explained, meaning the people in this area who shared a common language. "They lived in caves in the mountains. They came out maybe ten generations ago. Their cult objects were destroyed by missionaries, but a spirit carving named Pokiambut was hidden from the missionaries. It gives power to the clan."

While the flutists rested, two senior men brought Pokiambut into view. The carving emanated raw male power that was compelling. Long, deep curves defined a head with bulging brow, protruberant eyes and mouth, and a phallic projection below, while the head of a bird rose behind and above the humanoid head. Nestled in the base of the sculpture, a small stone carving looked very, very old.

Ancient stone carvings were rare, but Paul showed us another at Omblemas, one of the last accessible villages as the Arafundi River approached its headwaters in the forbidding central range.

"These people were the traditional enemies of Yimas," said Paul. "They moved here from the swamplands. There was no stone in the place they lived, and there is no stone here now. But they have a totem stone."

"How is that possible?" Bob asked.

"The answer is not known, but it is the totemic ancestor of the clan; it is called the Barong. It was created when the world was created. It has been in the same family from generation to generation. It is not allowed to bring the stone out of the *haus tambaran*. It is not to be brought into the sun or else the sun will turn yellow and the moon—no, the sun will turn red, the moon will turn yellow and the world will end."

We clambered into the spirit house, and from its dim recesses the totem was brought into view. A frayed, deep basket was gently opened to reveal a weathered carved stone circlet, cradled in a worn bailer shell. This Barong was a simple object. Yet gazing at it with its guardians, hovering at the edge of their collective memory, I shivered in the heat. Their need to envision what came before was intense. It seemed like my daughter's need, at the age of four or five, when she looked at me with a trusting gaze and asked urgently, "Where was I *before* I was born?" We all need continuities in our sense of being.

◈ ◈ ◈

Five others joined us in motoring downstream to board the *Sepik Spirit,* which would take us onto the great Sepik river. The ship was an arresting sight, its bridge surrounded by an expanse of glass that rose twelve feet to suggest the soaring facade of a *haus tambaran.* Yet we felt hermetically sealed—air-conditioned, protected from the heavy humidity and the whine and sting of insects, but shut off from the smells and sounds of the surround, especially the magic of bird-song at dusk and dawn.

But there were other wonders. As the ship's launch approached the village of Korogo, the crescent curve of a spirit house roof gleamed against the clouded sky. Then a huge face caught a shaft of morning sunlight. It was the gable ornament, surmounted by a soaring finial carved in the shape of a hornbill—a feminine symbol, as Paul's legend had told us. The sago siding was cut into scallops and carved spirit faces gazed out through openings between them. This *haus,* only five years old, was imbued with living spirit.

Several young men strutted among us as we sauntered toward the entrance. They were clad in trousers, but their torsoes were bare. Intricate designs composed of inch-long scars swirled up and down their backs, and flowed across their chests. These youths had been "eaten" by the crocodile in their initiation into manhood.

"You can take some photographs," Hubert, our younger guide, encouraged us. "You should each pay each man one *kina.* You see, there will be a large skin cutting this coming June, or maybe September. Forty-one boys are waiting," he added while the youths posed with obvious pride.

"Why would the boys want to do that?" wondered Leslie, one of our shipmates, when he was out of Hubert's earshot.

"Did you have a Bar Mitzvah?" I asked him. He had told us he was Jewish, and now he nodded.

"Isn't it somewhat the same?" I asked. As Leslie prepared for his Bar Mitzvah, he learned the beliefs of his people and confirmed his Jewish identity. Sepik youths learn the lore of their people and confirm their clan identity through initiation.

"Did you go through the skin cutting, Hubert?" Bob asked when we'd rejoined him again.

"Not yet," he said. "But I want to do it in my own village, Timbunke, when the new *haus tambaran* is finished—maybe this year. After that, I'll know the traditions of my clan."

"On the Karawari, the Christian church is strongly opposed to initiation," I told him. "Is that true here?"

"There's a Catholic Church in Korogo," Hubert said. "The men in the *haus* have already been to church this morning. But the priest here now is a national; he doesn't discourage the *tambaran* ceremonies. The priest before was European, and he didn't like it. And the other church, the Assembly of God, they don't like it either."

But it would happen. In the months between now and the initiation—we wished we could wait—there would be complex negotiations between the boys' fathers and other significant men. Responsibilities would be assigned and agreements reached about compensation for the rituals that would extend over many days.

Hubert led us into the lower level of the spirit house and up a ladder beneath the outspread legs of a carved female figure; in the upper story, boys were reborn as men. Huge eyes peered out from dark and grimy masks, obviously old. They had witnessed awful sights in the sacred enclosure—boys lying in prone across an inverted canoe or the supporting body of a man, writhing and moaning as hundreds of gashes were inflicted on their backs, buttocks, and thighs with bamboo knives as sharp as steel razors. The eyes had witnessed streaming blood and sweat, bathed away by each boy's mother's brother.

An awful sight. But in my mind's eye there was another awful sight—that image of a college fraternity initiate in the States, dumped alone, dead drunk, and naked into the snow at night. He didn't survive.

That was a meaningless death.

Here there was meaning. The bloodletting, which symbolized the "eating" of the boy by the ancestral crocodile spirit summoned from the river, cleansed the youth of the maternal essence he had ingested in the womb. The scarification, imprinting his skin with scale designs, imbued him with the crocodile's primal, masculine power.

"Come over here." It was Bob's voice; he had noticed two water drums. Hourglass-shaped with handles on top, they would be agitated up and down in water to produce the deep voices of ancestor spirits. When Bob raised his camera, an elderly man stepped forward and thrust out a warning hand. The artifacts up here were too sacred to be photographed, Hubert explained. In fact, this area was always under the vigilant protection of four senior men who slept in the four enclosures of mosquito netting near the walls.

Now that ancient and modern were colliding, the *haus* was both a sacred place and a market of art. The art of the Middle Sepik was world-renowned, and the ground level of the *haus tambaran* was a gallery of local work that was for sale. All the supporting posts and beams were intricately carved and elaborately painted. An entire tree trunk had been shaped into a massive bench; this was brought down from the old, abandoned *haus*. There were magnificent *garamut* drums, whose sculptures interwove human, avian, and reptilian figures in an orgy of imagination. Orator's stools had incised, bowed legs and a back composed of a carved figure with a small body and enormous head. The seats of the stools were thick, but they were not for sitting. In a gathering of males, each man wanting to display oratorical skills would stand by the stool and whack its seat with a switch to emphasize his important declarations.

We saw bundles of sacred flutes, and seven full-body masks. *Mwai* masks, these were called, with elliptical faces heavily bearded with tiny cowrie shells, and a crocodile or hornbill figure flowing down where an extended nose and out-thrust tongue might otherwise be. Masses of attached greenery and feathers comprised a cloak. During initiation, with drums booming and flutes intoning, these masks would be animated by hidden men. Moving in an ominous dance, they would awe, perhaps terrify, the boys. Dragging the boys into a vale of fear, helplessness, and humiliation was thought necessary before they could be masculinized.

Right now, men were lounging along *limbom* palm platforms on each side of the understory. Most of them looked fierce, with deeply creased, frowning faces. Yet when we stopped walking past them like carvings and talked to them like people, they were all good-natured—Leslie engaged one in an animated conversation.

"There are only men here," I mentioned to Hubert. "Where are the women?"

"Probably in their houses," he suggested. A pelting rain had begun.

"Do men here have more than one wife?"

"Yes, lots of men have two, some have three."

"So how many children might each man have?"

"Ten to fifteen. And almost all of the kids go to school," he volunteered. "It's a government school and the fee is five kina per year. The fee pushes people toward the cash economy."

Now the rain had become a deluge, and small, nude boys came out of the houses. Watching them cavort, some of the solemn men began to laugh. I had an impulse to strip down and join those children in their exuberant dance but the reaction might have been unwanted. So I waited until the downpour let up, then Leslie's wife and I meandered through the village. Sloshing through an inundated clearing, we reached a building where young men were gathered, and we heard the sounds of modern rock. A radio? A disco like Yimas Two? Hubert longed for an electronic bass, he'd told Bob. He played in two groups, high amp; they took their generator with them.

Julie and I couldn't see into the dimness, but sucking, smacking sexual sounds were directed toward us during a pause in the music. We turned back, feeling disheartened and demeaned.

◈ ◈ ◈

The other passengers disembarked at Timbunke, where there was an airfield, and the ship repositioned near the confluence of the

Korosameri and Blackwater rivers. Bob and I went exploring with Hubert and Wesley.

The khaki waters of the Korosameri borrowed the palest azure from the sky, but its glasslike calm was shattered by our outboard. Frightened birds erupted from the grasses—a flock of black grand manakins, swamp hens with blazing orange heads, a terra-cotta night heron that dropped its fish dinner as it frantically beat away. High above us, a masked harrier soared and swooped like an eagle, and there were eagles too. Many Papua New Guineans believed that birds embody the spirits of the dead. Today, I wished that our spirits could enter these creatures that glided on the rising currents of air.

Imperceptibly, the khaki waters had turned to ebony, nourished by tannin from the forests upstream. We were in the Blackwater River now, and distant peaks loomed above the morning mists. Bob and I gazed, caught by their mystery. Might there be people in those mountains whom Westerners hadn't yet encountered?

Then we were crashing through small floating grass islands. Hubert and Wesley stepped ashore and muscled us through by pulling the boat and pushing against the vegetation with supple, bare feet and grasping toes.

"You use your feet skillfully," I said to Hubert during a moment of rest. "You use your feet in ways we can't, since we keep ours enclosed in shoes." I meant it as a compliment, but the next day Hubert was wearing boots.

We'd seen his father's house in Timbunke, a large corrugated metal house with screened, louvered windows. He had been in Parliament for two terms, Hubert said, and now he was raising money to campaign for a third. He also also owned a trade store with Hubert's mother's brother—Bob bought batteries there. No wonder Hubert was self-conscious about bare feet, even if they served him well on the river.

The village and Catholic mission at Kaningara loomed high above the water. Sodden with sweat under a relentless sun, we trudged up a steep, clay path, passing corrugated metal buildings that felt like radiators as we went by.

"This is where the mission staff lives. There are two Australian nurses who run the health center—they've gone to Timbunke for supplies today—and the schoolteachers and their families," Wesley told us. "Two teachers are men and two are women, and the husband of one of the women has moved here too."

The classrooms, each a separate construction of palm and *pitpit*, were spread out along the path we were climbing. By a stroke of luck, our arrival coincided with a recess, and a male teacher appeared at the door of the topmost room as Bob and I approached.

"Good morning," Bob greeted him, explaining that we were travelers from the United States. "May we visit your class?"

"Yes indeed," the teacher responded, inviting us in with a gesture, and the milling children chorused "good morning" without coaching. A blackboard was in front of rows of simple desks and benches, with an outline of subjects being taught. "How to Become a Consumer" was the title of one.

"Do you receive world news?" Bob asked the teacher, noticing a short-wave radio on his desk.

"We do. You are Americans so I will tell you that these children were terrified when the Gulf War broke out. They thought the whole world would blow up. I was grateful when your President Bush stopped the bombing." His dark gaze impaled us. "I don't think a special interest such as oil should be allowed to put so many in danger all over the world."

"We agree," Bob said, and we fell silent, remembering those grim days when we questioned our leaders' motives.

"Is this your own village?" Bob asked after several minutes.

"Yes, but I went to Suva for my university education. I worry about the spread of violence in other countries. When I was in Fiji, I noticed a close connection between the introduction of violent videos—mostly from the United States—and the rise in violent crime. I very much fear that could happen in Papua New Guinea. But I wanted to come back here. These school buildings are cool and airy, and the villagers built a beautiful bush house for me. The metal buildings the other teachers live in are very hot."

Now it was time for classes to resume, so we continued our climb. At the crest of the hill, two Karawari figures a dozen feet tall commanded a sweeping view of river, marshes, and lakes. We'd seen such figures with Paul at a village named Amongabi Two. On either side of the entrance to an unused spirit house, a carved figure rose from the swirling waters. The curves of the heads, like those of Pokiambut, exaggerated the features of Melanesian men: a thrusting forehead that overhangs deeply set eyes and rises high on a sloping skull, a prominent nose that seems to curve toward the mouth, nostrils that flare obliquely away from the septum, deep creases that arc widely between nose and chin, and broad, full lips.

Below the heads, a series of crescents projected from a vertical support, like ribs jutting out from a spine. The upper ones curved down, the lower ones curved up, and at the center there was a protuberance—phallic on one figure, ambiguous on the other. The genital base of life?

Karawari Cult hooks, called Kamanggabi in the local language, were carved by the Arambak people who invoked their spiritual powers to shape major undertakings of the clan—warring raids, hunting expeditions, resettlement of a village. As the climax of an all-night *singsing,* the Big Man seized the most sacred Kamanggabi, whirled it rapidly above his head, and thrust it into the ground. Whichever direction the carving faced was the direction in which the clan must go. When the clan migrated, new Kamanggabis were carved and the spiritual power was transferred from the old into the new.

"Why are these Karawari figures here?" I asked Hubert. He didn't know, but our map provided an answer. The Karawari and Blackwater rivers flow in roughly parallel courses. It wasn't so far as the hornbill flies. "In the dry season, it might be possible to walk from here to the village of Amongabi," Hubert ventured.

Behind the Kamanggabi stood a Catholic Church. Its metal roof soared like a *haus tambaran,* supported by elaborately carved and painted pillars. Its finial ornament was an eagle. The church was open and filled with light, its pews (simple benches) arranged in five pie-shaped sections. Behind the altar—a wooden slab resting on carved columns—a Melanesian Christ with small body and elongated head drooped on a crucifix. Above and in front of the crucifixion, a carved bird was in flight. Christ's spirit escaping? Nearby, there was a Melanesian madonna and child carved from red kwila wood. Her mantle was adorned with another figure of a bird.

Two huge *garamut* drums stood by the choir. "We use them during the service," an elderly cleric watching us explained. "This is the new religion," he added enthusiastically. "The traditional beliefs and Christian beliefs come together here. The Christian God and our God, they are really the same."

Reluctantly moving on, we followed a track through the settlement along the ridge, passing steep trails leading down to a sago grove and to water. "They used to carry water up in bamboo containers," Hubert told us. "Now plastic buckets are used." At this elevation of a few hundred feet, the air was fresher and there were no mosquitoes. "All the villages used to be this high so that people could watch for the approach of an enemy."

A new spirit house was under construction here. Men had floated huge logs to the base of the hill, and then muscled them up. Carved uprights over thirty feet tall, portraying stunningly virile males, were already in place. Some of the uprights had clan names carved in them, explained a nearby white-haired elder who was wearing a large pair of boar's tusks around his neck and yellow cotton trousers. The names designated areas of the *haus* to be used by particular clans. Seven clans lived in this village, and they all would be coming together in one *haus tambaran*, he told us proudly.

"Okay to take pictures?" asked Bob, and the answer was "yes" if he would pay one kina for each picture.

"Agreed." Bob said, although the price was steep. Maybe he was remembering Conrad's statement that travelers help keep traditions alive.

"How many people in the village?" Bob asked when he was finished.

"Maybe three hundred now," Wesley said. This village was three or four generations old, the elder added, explaining that it was established, maybe, in the 1930s. These clans had lived in the hills, but the Australians urged them to move to the rivers to get supplies and to make it easier for the patrols. Two clan leaders got seven clans to cooperate in moving to this area. The posts at each end of the *haus* represented the clans of those leaders.

"Is this spirit house connected with the Catholic church?" I asked and the answer was "no," this was a traditional *haus* with no connection to the church. Questions crowded my mind but it was time to leave—we had to rendezvous with the *Sepik Spirit* before dark.

"Do most people on the river believe that there is only one God, and that the human spirit goes to heaven after death?" I asked Wesley as we passed the Catholic church.

"Few are convinced that that there is only one spirit that goes to heaven," he said gravely. "They believe in other spirits that inhabit the bush." He walked in silence for a few moments, and then he spoke again.

"Those spirits have been heard. They have also been seen."

I was ready to be persuaded.

UNDERSTANDING

◇

Chapter Thirteen

REUNION WITH PIRIP

While the children of Kaningara recovered from their terror that the world would blow up because of Operation Desert Storm, Bob and I were recovering from our bleak alienation. Shafts of light began piercing the dark clouds over our country as election time approached.

Our new home state was a testing ground and, as candidates zoomed through, we shook live hands and asked live questions and took the measure of would-be Big Men from several yards away. And when new leaders were elected, our sense of hope was reignited.

But what about my icon of change, my dark-skinned sister across the world? I wrote to Pirip several times, but there was no answer. Had she lost interest in communicating with me? Was she ill? Bob and I planned one more trip, I sent off one more letter and we simply hoped.

By October of 1993 we were at Haus Poroman, the "house of friends," near Mt. Hagen. At 6,500 feet, it was sited at Kuta Ridge, above the creek where the Australian prospector, Michael Leahy, thought he had found a Wahgi Valley El Dorado in 1933. He had not; the yield of gold was modest. But, preserving the family connection, the small lodge was owned by Maggie Wilson, a daughter of the youngest Leahy brother, Dan, and her Australian husband, Keith. We had barely settled into a cozy bungalow when there was a knock on the door.

"You have visitors," announced one of the staff, and in walked Pirip and another woman. Without a word, Pirip hugged me tightly, keening, sobbing, warm tears dripping from her cheeks and trickling down my neck. It was a long intense hug that bridged the four-year separation.

Pirip, whose speech now flowed easily back and forth between pidgin and English, explained that she did receive my letter and had ridden the PMV from Minj to Mt. Hagen and caught a ride up to Haus Poroman. Maggie Wilson promised to drive her back. Although I could understand much of Pirip's pidgin, her companion, who spoke fluent English, acted as translator when we needed her. This was yet another of the plethora of Elizabeths who had been associated with Pirip—Elizabeth Konmil (Kupul), she wrote in my notebook. Kupul was her husband's name.

"I've been working with Pirip," she explained. "The women didn't cooperate with her, so she let other groups begin using the *haus win*."

"I'm very happy to see you both, but we had no idea you might come here today. We're going to visit you in Minj tomorrow."

"That will be a good day to visit," Pirip said. "It is Tuesday. Tuesday is a working day when the subdistrict presidents will be meeting."

"What kind of work do you do when you meet?" I inquired.

"Discuss plans," she answered. "The presidents, they bring money from their groups—they bring ten kina each week from selling their crops."

"We want you to read this," Elizabeth broke in, handing me a typed page. "We want you to read it now."

PROFILE FOR MRS. PIRIP KURU
South Waghi Center:
Minj District from 1974 to 1993

Mrs. Pirip Kuru has become an active member of the Women's Club in 1974 when it was first established.

From 1974, she was elected President of Minj District Women's Council. She represents about thirty women's groups in the Western Highlands Provincial Women's Council.

From 1984, she was elected to represent 13 other District Presidents in the Western Highlands Provincial Women's Council.

In 1986, she was elected to become Western Highlands Provincial Women's Council Treasurer.

At the moment, she is active for women's rights and to bring new development to upgrade women's living standards in general.

She has contributed a lot of effort to assist the women of Western Highlands to fight for their rights and voice their grievances to their male counterparts. Women are finally enjoying some privileges now.

Because of her and a few other women in the Province who had to struggle hard for the sake of other sisters, the Provincial Government of Western Highlands has finally endorsed and approved their Five Year Women's Development Programme.

To implement the programme the WHP Government has allocated grants to the women since 1989.

She has contributed a lot to assist our women so she should be given recognition in this Village Services Scheme and be given a position to see that the women in the District get better services through her network.

She has been working for the past twenty years on a voluntary basis for the betterment of women of the Western Highlands.

She has done a lot for the women of the Province and because of her constant struggle for her women folks betterment, she now has been recognized by the National Women's Council and she is presented with this Service Medal.

"You've done fine work," I said to Pirip, who had been watching me closely, and her eyes gleamed with pleasure. "But I still wonder what caused you to start this work. Let's sit and talk for a little while, then Bob and I are going for a trek. The guide is waiting." I motioned Pirip and her companion toward one of the beds, I settled on the other, and Bob went off to ask the guide if he could wait.

"You once told me that your parents put you in a mission school when you were maybe seven or eight years old," I reminded Pirip, and she nodded. "You were a little girl and I've been wondering, were you sad to leave your family then or were you happy?"

"Happy. I loved school so I wanted to go," she declared.

"You didn't feel sad to leave your mum?" I persisted—a mum myself, and once a girl who had longed for a loving mum.

"Did not feel sad," Pirip said firmly. Her father loved her and didn't want her to go to school, she added. She usually did what he told her to do—breaking firewood, fetching water, taking care of the pigs. He wanted her to stay home to do that work, but she was tired of it, so she left and went to school.

"Was it customary at that time for a girl to be sent to school?" I asked. Now Pirip spoke at length to Elizabeth.

"Pirip's saying, 'When the missionary came we saw that it was interesting—missionary and school, it was all interesting. That is why we went, me and my brothers, into school.'"

"Did your father have to pay money—school fees?"

"Free school," Pirip said. "At that time, there were no money. They use kina shells, feathers, this was the valuables."

"Of course," I said, feeling foolish. "I really knew that. But your father did not have to give valuables, is that right?"

"Not needed," Pirip declared, and then spoke so fast that I turned to Elizabeth for help again. I asked her to try to use Pirip's own words.

"Pirip says, 'I did my elementary in 1955 and did my grade one to three in the following year. At school I was selected as the girls' school captain.'" Her responsibilities included helping the students with their work, searching for students who ran away from school, and then bringing them back, Elizabeth explained.

"Pirip says the missionary trusted her because she was bright and brave enough to carry out her responsibilities as the girls' captain. Later they told her to carry mail from Mondimal Station—the mission was there—to Minj. At that time there were no roads up there so she walked from Mondimal to Minj, posted the mail, and took back the incoming mail from Minj to Mondimal. That was her favorite duty."

"At Christmas every year," Pirip broke in eagerly, "I usually get present for the hard work and as a bright student at school. My parents also get presents for the hard work I have done at school. My father gets a hat and for Mum they give her clothes. I was happy in all the schoolwork I have done and also in how the missionary treated me."

"Only one missionary or more?" I asked.

"Many. The first time the missionaries came there were three men—Swiss Evangelical. Later they send missionary's girl friend; they send her from Germany, and when missionary and girl friend got married I was flower girl." Pirip's face glowed with pleasure.

"You were really special!" I said and she returned my smile. "Pirip, did the missionaries think that some of the old traditions were good or not?"

"Not. They stop all the traditional ways." Uneasily, I recalled my early letter criticizing missionaries for suppressing local beliefs— what may she have thought of that?

"Well, I can see that you were already a leader even when you were a girl," I said with a surge of nostalgia for my own school—a girl's day school—where I too, had been a hard worker and good student and had won prizes. But now Bob brought me back to the present, signaling from the doorway. "Unfortunately, Bob and I have to go out now," I told the women. "When will Maggie take you back to Mt. Hagen?"

"We want to stay and look around at this place first," Elizabeth explained. "Maggie says she might be able to help us get guests to stay in our *Haus Win.*" So we parted ways, agreeing to meet at the roadside near Pirip's home around ten the next day.

◈　◈　◈

Early in the morning, we started out with Agua, the guide who had driven us in 1989. Bob and he fell into easy conversation.

"Do you have a family now, Agua?" Bob asked.

"Yes, I have two children, two months and two years of age. They live with their mother among my people, up there, high in the mountains." Agua pointed toward the Kumpor range that bounds the valley to the south. "I have a van now, and I go up to stay with them on weekends."

"You've been working for the agency for several years. Has that work changed your life?" Agua's face creased with pleasure.

"If I did not work for wages, we would not have things we have like a car, better clothes, better education." Agua had four years of schooling.

"Is cash bringing in any problems?" Bob asked, and Agua looked grim.

"In Hagen, there is much gambling, drinking beer, even raping women. Some men are making homemade guns from pipes."

"When did that begin?"

"It is since about 1985. A man will get someone with a license— maybe a policeman—to buy ammunition. They pay fifty kina, which they steal. And not long ago, the post office caught some guns coming through the post. They traced them to a missionary; he was importing guns."

"To sell?" I asked in horror. Agua shook his head and shrugged.

"I do not know the reason," he said, and we all fell silent.

Pirip was waiting at the roadside when we approached her place in Minj. The lane into her homestead was freshly cleared and decorated with patterns of black stones. As we turned in, four generations of her family surged toward us: her husband, Kuru, and his mother; Stanley, the youngest son; and Gertrude, the younger daughter with her son. The warmth of their welcome enfolded me.

Then Pirip's second oldest son, Mike, sauntered by. About five-and-a-half feet tall, muscular and slim, he sported mirrored sunglasses, a cap with the bill turned backwards, an inch-long pigtail, a T-shirt with Samur beach (a tourist beach in Bali) emblazoned on the front, sweat pants, sneakers, and a large, fancy digital watch. He looked like the epitome of Joe Cool, but he sounded like a thoroughly nice kid as he hovered near Bob.

"Are you in school?" Bob asked—this was Tuesday morning.

"I've finished eighth grade, and I have two more years in secondary school," Mike said. "But I'm taking a year out of school to help with mama Pirip's work—she needs help. I like life in the highlands, but I'm unhappy that my sisters were both mistreated."

"Both sisters? Ruth told us last year that Gertrude was beaten by her husband and they were going to try for a divorce."

"That's true," Mike said. "They are divorced."

"Did something happen to Ruth too?" asked Bob.

"Yes, she and Chris are separated. He's in Madang with a younger woman. Myself, I won't marry until I'm twenty-five."

"Is that the usual age for marriage?" Bob asked and Mike nodded.

"Most younger men are no good," he asserted. "They do nothing. They're not married, they don't have any work. They just play around—they play darts, they drink beer."

"But women sure do work," Bob said, his attention caught by a snowfall of feathers where two women were plucking chickens. Others were peeling sweet potato—*kaukau*—and arranging bananas, fleshy beans, and various greens on a large, blue plastic sheet, preparing a feast. Four years before, our feast had been cooked in a traditional earth oven. Today, women were laying moist banana leaves over hot stones in a sawed-off oil drum, layering in chicken parts, vegetables, and a slab of pig fat brought by one of the presidents.

Four buildings stood in the compound now—the *haus win,* the sleeping house for women and children, and two houses under construction. One would be a guest house, Pirip explained, and one would be "for teaching and projects." The larger building had been framed for four windows, and sheets of woven siding leaned against a wall. "The Association does not have money to complete the buildings yet," she said.

She urged her family and the ten presidents who had come today into the *haus win* to talk. Artifacts were displayed on the walls—*bilums,* necklaces made of seeds and beads, the copper pendant I left as a gift in 1992. A poster urged breast feeding as the healthy way.

Money was Pirip's agenda. In 1984, she told us, the national government gave a grant to the provincial government for women's programs, but the money went into the pockets of politicians (this had already happened once before we met in 1983). In 1986, another grant came to the province. But there were fourteen districts and twenty-two subdistricts that had to divide the money. "Little came to us. Could you help us get money from the American government? I know it gives money to people in other countries."

"I don't know how to do that," I said regretfully, explaining that aid went first to countries in which people were dying of starvation and disease. Pirip looked down, her shoulders sagging. I leaned closer and put an arm around her shoulders; she didn't pull back. "You look so sad it makes me sad. Think of how much you've done since I was here before. You have an association working together."

"But I plan to build *three* houses," Pirip declared urgently. "It is very important to have buildings so people can see what has been done. I have been working for women for so long." Her voice faltered and she slumped in dejection.

"Yes you have, and you should feel proud of what you've done. When we go to Moresby, I'm going to meet the sister of the Ambassador to the United States," I said. "I'm told that she and the Ambassador are both very interested in women's needs. Would you like me to talk with her about your work and see if she could help?" Pirip pondered for a few moments.

"It is too soon," she said. "Maybe later on."

"Then tell me this—what changes do the women in your association want to make in their lives now?"

"The most important aim is for women to make choices, not be ruled by men," Pirip said, her voice spirited again.

Then Elizabeth chimed in. "I want to teach literacy in the new center. And I want to build a shelter for deserted women. Nowadays, a deserted woman is shamed—her family may blame her if her husband leaves her."

"Literacy and shelters are very important, and we'll talk more about those things later. But tell me now, what are the good things in women's lives, what would you all *not* want to change?" I'd never asked Pirip that question before. My glimpses of river life had brought it into focus, seeing past pulled into present in creative ways.

After a thoughtful silence, several women began to talk while Pirip and Elizabeth translated their words.

"We have freedom to work or not to work."

"The family takes care of each other."

"We always have food."

"We would not change keeping pigs. Pigs are very important, like money, for celebrations, for bride-price. Women are responsible for the pigs."

I wished I could write those words on an enormous poster and mount it on the wall—or even the roof! Knowing so little of life in other lands, these women had no idea of the importance of what they told me.

WE HAVE FREEDOM TO WORK OR NOT TO WORK.

THE FAMILY TAKES CARE OF EACH OTHER.

WE ARE RESPONSIBLE FOR THE VALUABLES (THE PIGS).

WE ALWAYS HAVE FOOD.

Just then, women carried in large aluminum pots full of food, and banana leaves were passed out as plates. Bob and I had enjoyed our previous *mumus*—the steamed vegetables were moist and tasty, and, in the decade since our first visit, our own low-fat, "heart-healthy" meals had become similar to the highlanders' traditional diet. But today, as a sign of women's growing prosperity, every morsel was unctuous with pig fat. Grease slimed my mouth and oozed down my chin as I ate a *kaukau*, washing it down with gulps of canned soda that Mike brought from the trade store. The women were chatting and laughing as they ate, and I hoped none of them noticed.

When we stood up at the end of the meal, Pirip moved awkwardly and clutched her knee.

"Do you have a problem with your knee?" I asked.

"She has a problem with her weight," Elizabeth said with a laugh. I found it hard to smile—on their traditional diet, the active highlanders were lean. And later on, when Pirip asked about our travel plans and I mentioned trekking in the remote Schrader Mountains, it was disheartening to hear her say, "I do not walk in the mountains any more."

The afternoon was waning, so we began our good-byes. We exchanged warm hugs and then, with stinging eyes, we turned and drove away.

Chapter Fourteen

FRESH PERSPECTIVES

A year later, a heap of crumpled newspapers reminded me of that discussion of Kuma traditions in Pirip's *haus win*. On a weekend retreat from the bleakness of November in New Hampshire, Bob and I welcomed the sunrise from the fifth floor of a New York City hotel. As I gazed across Central Park, where golden leaves still clung to the Norway maples, a pile of papers on a park bench began to quiver. An arm in a ragged sleeve emerged, then came shoulders. A head covered with long, stringy gray hair began shaking away the dregs of uneasy slumber—or was the person shivering as she gathered her rags into a bundle?

Did she (or he—it was hard to be sure) have enough food to eat? Did she have the choice to work or not to work? Was she taken care of by her family? Did she control any valuables? And what about her shelter—a cocoon of rags and newspapers on a cold city street? PNG highland bush huts, smoky from the everglowing fires, were much more comfortable than that; Bob and I had slept in them while we trekked in the mountains.

I wrote to Pirip in early December, describing that city scene of apparent despair, as well as a few other weak seams in US society. Then I encouraged her again to be mindful of the positive elements in Kuma culture even as she worked toward change.

◈ ◈ ◈

After writing, I let thoughts chase each other across my mind. There had been a sea change in my concern for those women in 1993, when my questions shifted from change to preservation, and it took a year to fathom why that happened.

It happened because I was enchanted by the wholeness of

Karawari river life—the floating market was emblematic—as well as the fact that women's traditional work seemed to be as highly valued as men's. And it happened because of the creative integrations of old and new we saw on the Sepik and Blackwater rivers. Young men needing to affirm their masculinity and clan identity in a rapidly changing world were reclaiming ancient rites of initiation. Yet spirit houses and Christian churches were coexisting, meeting some of the challenges of transition.

But there was more to my shift of perspective.

At home, I had been interviewing movers for another book, and reached a new understanding of my own flawed transition. Saying good-bye to special people, special places, special doings had swamped me when we left New Haven. I couldn't endure the sadness, so I severed my connections. I didn't visit, I didn't write, I didn't even phone.

I replayed old tapes in reverse. My early life was littered with leavings.

The leaving of a comforting English nanny sailing back to her home—Chepstow, wherever that might be. When we walked down the gangplank of the ocean liner that would take her away, I let out a frantic bark of laughter; it erupted instead of a sob. A big girl who's three years old doesn't cry, they said.

The leaving of a man enslaved by scotch and soda, who could be neither father nor husband. Maybe he couldn't bear to be himself.

The leaving of a mother demolished by the final rejection of divorce; she lost her mind and never entirely found it again.

The leaving of a sister cursed with a paternal gene, who drowned in her alcoholic vomit one night. Her heart stopped beating when she was forty-four.

Stark endings. Final endings. Endings I couldn't prevent.

True, holding the warm, strong hand of a man named Bob—nanny, father, and mother as well as friend and lover—I grew a splendid new life. But when its thousand fragile roots were torn loose by our move, when the sadness, confusion, fury, and longing lying dormant from the earlier leavings fired up to meld with the sadness, confusion, fury, and longing from the new one, I curled inward and stiffened like a dry pandanus leaf. But that didn't work at all.

I wanted to convey my new awareness to the women of Minj, to women everywhere. I wanted to say, "When you make a big change, don't turn your back on the past and cut yourself adrift from people and places and roles that matter. Stay connected, pull the positive elements forward with you."

If I had said all that in the 1993 meeting, would the women have been mystified? Or might they intuitively have understood?

◈ ◈ ◈

19 April 1995

Dear Pirip and Elizabeth,

I wrote to you in December but no answer has come. I am close to finishing my book about Papua New Guinea. It will say a lot about you and the struggles of women to change your lives, and I would like to share with you any future earnings from the book. But I still need to understand more about why you began this work.

Bob and I would like to see you again. It would be between 5 and 10 November. If you would like to see us again, please write as soon as you receive this letter.

Please give our good wishes to your fine families.

My love to you,
Audrey

◈ ◈ ◈

8 May 1995

Dear Audrey & Bob,

Thank you very much for your nice letter which I received today. I'm very sorry to hear that you didn't receive my last letter to you.

The round house built when you were here is completed, and there's another one similar to that with three rooms. Pirip is living in it until our group can find money to get bedding, stove, eating utensils for our guests. We have put up fencing but it's only half completed.

The group raised K2,500 for the fence and still need K5,000 more to complete the whole area. The first house we built is now used as our office & meeting place.

Last year New Zealand High Commissioner allocated 2 million kina to women & youth groups in PNG. So we got the application forms from the Agricultural Bank of PNG and I help my women in each group fill in all the details the bank needs. Since the beginning of this year each group is entitled to get K2,000 each. We have thirty-five groups in our association and each of the groups has ten members so altogether there are 350 members.

The first loan was released last year April and only fourteen groups got the loan and twenty-one groups will get theirs next month. The women are quite busy now with their own small projects such as:

Piggery

Poultry

Trade stores

Sewing

Selling secondhand clothing

Betel nut selling

Coffee

So the whole idea is that we want our women to know how to earn their own money, look after the family well and live in good houses. Besides that they can have a little money to contribute to our centre.   I think that's all I have to say and maybe some more next time

Bye for now—we love you,

from Elizabeth & Pirip [written in Elizabeth's handwriting]

◈ ◈ ◈

16 May 1995

Dear Audrey McCollum,

Hello and thank you very much for the letter that we have received last Christmas. It took us so long to reply because . . . Elizabeth was in Port Moresby. Mum waited for her and that took her a long time, so mum she told me to write the reply letter. . . .

Anyway we are very glad that in your last letter you mentioned all the stories that we have shared during our small meeting in the *haus win*. Mum and I, we greatly thought of how you memorize the culture, the life style of our people, how pigs are valuable and other things. As you know, these traditions will not change. . . . The Women's Association is doing fine with their work.

[She repeats the news about the grant].

The literacy work has been done last year but it was not successful so they put a stop to it. We believe that this year the literacy work will be successful because the women are cooperating with each other. . . . Mum took her share of the loan money and we built a small trade store at the junction. . . .

Yours Faithfully,
Pirip Til Kuru
Son: Nombri Michael Kuru.

I answered Elizabeth's letter promptly before Michael's letter arrived, explaining that we would like to return to Minj in November if Pirip would definitely be there. I asked for confirmation.

◈ ◈ ◈

Undated—received July 15

Dear Audrey McCollum,

Hello and thank you very much for the third letter that I have received on the date 23 June. . . . I am really happy and grateful that you have written a book about your travel in New Guinea and have said that the story is mainly about me. How dear you have done this. . . . it is really hard for me to tell you how I feel in myself about the book and also thanks very much for your sharing of what you will earn from the book, I mean the contribution towards the women's centre. . . .

The women's centre is known to all the community and also is known throughout our province. That makes me really proud of it.

[She repeats the information about the grant.] So now we have increased the members in the group. The group meeting is held as usual, the literacy work . . . is programmed for next year.

I am really happy that you and Bob want to see us again. I'll be really happy to see you in New Guinea.

I was very sick at the beginning of this year. The doctor that examined me said that I have four different sick and they give me medicine and my sick was finished but the swollen knees are still paining. Also I have heart ache and sometimes I have strong headache so if you think you can make an effort to find other medicines for me please do so.

Best wishes from me and my family to all of yours.

Yours faithfully,
Pirip Til Kuru
Son: Michael Kuru Kayeson

Two xeroxed sheets from the Nazarene Hospital were enclosed. Pirip's symptoms were headache, dizziness, swelling, and tenderness of the knee. Although chloroquine and codeine were prescribed, Bob saw no evidence of malaria. At the bottom of the sheet, Michael wrote this:

NB. Mum was very sick. She has four different types of sick. The doctor examined her and said that the sick was in the nerves . . . Know that she is very sick. She needs some medicine so if you have medicine for the above mentioned sick, please kindly send some of the medicine that will cure her. Thanks and this is all.

Bob and I had vacillated about the trip because the planning was so complex, but that letter clinched it. If Pirip was in danger, we would go.

◈ ◈ ◈

15 June 1995

Dear Pirip and Michael,

Bob and I are very sorry to learn that you, Pirip, are sick. If we knew what medicines to send that would help you, of course we would do that. But Bob, who is a doctor, studied the report from the hospital, and there is not enough information. The doctor thought you might have malaria, you might have typhoid fever, or the problems might be caused by nerves. The doctor suggested three medicines, and we suppose that you have used them. Bob does not know what medicine he could send that would help you. If you take the wrong medicine, that could do you harm. One of the medicines, codeine, cannot be sent through the mail. That is against the law in our country. We do hope that by the time this letter reaches you, you will be feeling well again.

We are coming back to PNG if we can see you and your family. It will be between 5 November and 15 November. Nombri Michael, could you please write as soon as possible and tell us if Pirip will be in Minj at that time? If you take the reply coupon I have enclosed to the post office, they will exchange it for stamps, so you won't have to spend your own money.

Bob joins me in sending our love to you and your fine family,
Audrey

Mike wrote to confirm that Pirip would be in Minj when we arrived.

◈ ◈ ◈

Haus Poroman felt like a sanctuary after another grueling 10,000 mile journey. At day's end, Bob and I lounged by the circular stone fireplace that centered the oval main building, then the side door opened and a woman walked in.

"Good evening. I'm Maggie," she said with a radiant smile. Her skin was paler than Pirip's, more like coffee-and-cream. Her walnut brown hair formed a halo around her face, with a few tendrils softening the high slope of her forehead. Her gaze was direct and guileless. She led us to an oblong dining table covered with tapa cloth and sat across from Bob and me on one of the fat upended logs that served as seats.

"I'm delighted to meet you at last," I told Maggie Wilson, the owner of Haus Poroman. I had faxed her from home, saying that I hoped to talk with her about highland women's changing lives. As Barbara, who seemed to be manager of operations, quietly served our meal, I told Maggie about my relationship with Pirip, and my plan to visit her the next day.

"In one of their letters, Elizabeth and Pirip wrote that there was a grant from the New Zealand government for loans to Papua New Guinea women, but I don't quite understand how it works."

"It's administered through the Women's Division of the Ministry of Home Affairs," Maggie explained. Although Bob and I were alone with Barbara and Maggie, her voice was so soft I had to strain to hear.

"Is the minister a woman?"

"No. There are no women ministers," said Maggie ruefully. "The minister is a man, but the head of that division is a woman."

"I've heard that it's hard for officials in Moresby to understand the needs of rural highland women. Do you think that's true for this woman?"

"Well, she's a highland woman herself," was Maggie's ambiguous answer. "But I saw the president of the National Council of Women this weekend in Moresby, and she's discouraged about making progress for women through the government."

While I tackled my lavish serving of beef, with carrots, green beans, and white potatoes from Maggie's garden, she told me about the grant. Each loan could be up to 500 kina, with a low rate of interest, and was supposed to be repaid within two or three years.

"I thought the application form was too complex. I made some suggestions about how it could be simplified."

"Were your suggestions accepted?" Maggie's half smile was her reply.

"Are you with the Provincial Council of Women?" I asked.

"I was the president of the Western Highlands Province Council for six years, then I decided I could be more effective working independently and helping others. I've also been an advisor at national meetings." Maggie had recently been trying to get government endorsement of smaller lodges to encourage interaction between guests and local people. "I want tourists to gain a true understanding of local people."

"Tell me, then, if my impression is accurate. It's seemed to me that many women are losing influence as the country is developed."

"I agree with that. Traditional women had great power—the women controlled the pigs and therefore controlled the men." Maggie glanced at Bob, as though wondering how he would react to that, but his expression apparently reassured her. "Women could refuse to relinquish the pigs for male purposes. Men feared the strength of women, they resented women's pregnancy and childbirth, so some highland men went through scarification to prove their own strength and tolerance of pain.

"Westerners misconstrue bride-price, you know. They think it means women are objects to be sold. They see our women with their *bilums* filled and they think, 'poor things.' They encourage women to feel that way too. I encourage rural women to see themselves as strong, to feel proud that they can carry such big loads." Maggie's shoulders and neck straightened as she spoke, and her voice was spirited now.

"I'm afraid I was one of those outsiders who thought 'poor things,'" I confessed. "But my ideas have changed in twelve years— now I worry about the fast push into the cash economy. Sure, the whole world's been moving that way, but that isn't solving human problems. Let me tell you about a conversation I had with Pirip and some Minj women in 1993. Until then, I'd always asked what they hoped to change in their lives. This time I asked what they wanted to preserve, and their answers amazed me." I recounted to Maggie the four shining aspects of life that those women didn't want to change.

"We can't say those things about a lot of women in the States. They don't all have enough food to eat; they can't decide when they want to work and when they don't; they don't all have family to look after them; they don't necessarily control the valuables." And I told Maggie about poverty, loneliness, and homelessness in the United States.

"We don't think enough about what we do have," Maggie said soberly.

"That's true of us all," I answered as Maggie abruptly left the table and walked toward the fireplace. She lit a cigarette and I realized she was shielding us from the smoke. But as she moved around restlessly, looking pensive, I wondered if I had upset her. Then she flicked the butt into the fire and came back to the table.

"You have caused me to think deeply," she said. "But cash is necessary to get things done. You can't even protect the environment without cash."

"Yes and no," I thought, but decided that was too complex for now.

"My dream is not only success in business, but it connects with how I'll use the money." Maggie's eyes were sparkling as she described some of her ideas: a center in Moresby to demonstrate the making of traditional crafts; a program "for wives of business men who live behind barricades in Moresby." We had seen the barricades that had sprouted up in a dozen years—chain-link fences or masonry walls topped with razor wire. Worse than Los Angeles or New Haven, where the have-nots rage against the haves? Or more tragic? That razor wire slashed not only flesh; it slashed cultures into fragments of disconnection.

"Rich men invest their money in other countries," Maggie went on. "I believe women would invest their money in Papua New Guinea. Here's an example. There's a woman who runs a sawmill; she asks 'If the timber is going to be cut, why should it go to Asia?' And I, myself, have been training women to run lodges such as the Haus Poroman."

"I think Pirip talked with you about her guest house when she was here in 1993," I reminded Maggie.

"Yes she did. I've known Pirip a long time and I get on with her well. I asked her to consider how she could provide what Westerners would want—I told her it would take at least five years to develop a lodge. Pirip has said nothing more about it."

"I'd like your advice, Maggie." I told her about my book and explained my wish to share any future royalties with Pirip and her association. I planned to make an advance donation tomorrow, and there seemed a sweet logic in earmarking that for literacy training.

"That's a beautiful idea," Maggie said quietly. "But I think a literacy program works only if the women are really motivated to learn. The government will supply a teacher if the village supplies housing, some payment for supplies, and if they show motivation. Perhaps it would be best to leave the decision to the women, and only recommend that your donation be used for literacy.

"I'd like to read your book," Maggie went on. "I've wanted to write a book myself, but I need someone to help me get started." Maggie's life had been suspended between two worlds she explained as we moved closer to the fire. She was the daughter of one of the Leahy brothers—an Australian gold prospector—and a highland woman, and was now the wife of an Australian expatriate. Her formal education involved several years in Australia.

"I was an outstanding athlete and I had many friends, but there was prejudice too. My Australian family provided for me well, but they were cold," she said wistfully, her eyes looking like a bewildered child's. "My mother's people were very warm but, as the child of a mixed marriage, I was sometimes lonely. My mother's father was very important to me, he paid a lot of attention to me—I even spent time in the men's house."

"Is that common?" I asked. Pirip had said the same thing.

"Oh yes. Highland men have traditionally been involved with their children and grandchildren. My two sisters are back in our village now, and I enjoy my connection with the village very much." Then we talked about writing books until Bob and I began to sag—our day had begun before dawn.

Chapter Fifteen

THE CIRCLE BEGINS CLOSING

Pirip was on the move the next morning. "Come with me," she said after a surge of welcome had swirled around us—smiles, hugs, and handshakes from Pirip, Gertrude, Kuru, his mother, and women in the district association who had come for their meeting. Carrying a towel, toothbrush, and toothpaste, she led me through gardens to a small creek, with Bob and Elizabeth Konmil trailing behind. "This is where the washing up is done," she told me (her English was interspersed with pidgin now, rather than the reverse, and it was slightly less formal). She then hurried to a pool where the stream had been dammed.

"Pirip had this constructed to hold water coming down from the mountain springs," Elizabeth explained. Standing knee deep, Pirip brushed her teeth vigorously and began to sluice down and soap her clothed body.

"She wants to take her clothes off," Elizabeth said, glancing at Bob.

"I'll tell him," I reassured her, "although Bob's a doctor and he's seen a lot of bodies."

"A doctor, he sees everything," Pirip chimed in, but I called to Bob that Pirip was going to bathe and he turned his back. Pirip pulled off her *meri* blouse and skirt and stood in the water in a half slip, sunshine gleaming on her full breasts and round belly—a brown-skinned Rubens nude, her nakedness presaging other disclosures to come.

"She's too fat," Elizabeth chuckled. "When she went into the hospital in January the doctor said she's too fat, so she's lost some weight but not enough. She's feeling better now, though she still has trouble with her knees." Pirip, ignoring her friend's remarks, soaped her hair, arms, chest, and legs, rinsed with splashes of water from the pool, and then wrapped herself in a towel.

"Do you drink the water here?" I asked.

"No, that comes from farther along," she said. "I'll show you." We made our way through a grove of coffee trees, their leaves lustrous with health, and arrived at a small cascade flowing over a pandanus leaf spout.

Elizabeth had waved to Bob to rejoin us, and Pirip led us across the stream and through abundant gardens. Cleanly dug drainage ditches laced the black soil in which corn, onions, pumpkins, greens, sugar cane, taro, and three kinds of *kaukau* were growing. Pigs rooted in a fallow area, and, nearby, a raised earthen grave was sheltered by a metal roof.

"Kuru's father," Pirip said casually, and it seemed natural that he slumbered on in the family land.

"The gardens look bigger than I remembered," I said, glancing toward the casuarina trees that defined the boundaries. Both women nodded.

"Pirip's family is even lending some land to another family to grow peanuts," Elizabeth volunteered.

"Did you have all this land before?" I asked. Pirip nodded again and explained that more was under cultivation now, since more family were here to help. Her older son John was living here with his bride, and son Mike was here too—he finished tenth grade last week. He was waiting for the results from an examination to find out if he could go to technical school. "Or maybe university," she added proudly.

"Where's the rest of the family?" I inquired, and learned that Stanley, now eleven and in fourth grade, was living in Madang with Ruth and Chris.

"Mike told us they were separated," I said.

"Chris didn't pay the bride-price, so we sent him away," Pirip explained matter-of-factly. "Then I allowed him to come back in the family."

"And Gertrude?

"She's divorced and she lives with us now."

More people had gathered. Pirip led us back past the familiar *haus bilong slip*—this was where John, his new wife, and Kuru slept, she said.

"I thought Kuru slept in the men's house," I told her.

"That's finished," she said curtly (Bob heard otherwise from her sons later in the day), then she ushered us into her own new sleeping house. Behind the main room where we entered, there were two smaller rooms. One held a wooden bed with a sapphire blue coverlet; wall hooks supported *bilums* and clothing. "My room," she said. Mike slept in the other, and Stanley slept in a small alcove when he was home. Another alcove by the entry held a small kerosene stove and several utensils.

While Pirip dressed in a fresh *meri* blouse and wrapped skirt, I surveyed the main room. Above a table displaying five large shells and a bowl of pineapple, a bulletin board was pinned with photos Bob had taken of Pirip with me, my letters to her, and two large prints of an alabaster-white Jesus. They held my eye. Were I to paint Jesus here, I would have chosen as my model a man walking on the road this morning. He was ebony black and the sunlight behind him made a halo of his bushy white hair.

"Come," said Pirip, leading us into a new traditional-style building for the meeting. Bob and I joined the others sitting in a circle on woven grass mats—we were no longer enthroned on chairs. Pirip, the district president, opened the meeting with a pidgin prayer, then conducted a roll call in an authoritative tone. Although there were fifteen group presidents and an additional half dozen women and several men, she looked stern when she finished and spoke rapidly in pidgin.

"She says there's not a quorum so we can't do official business," Elizabeth explained. Then Pirip introduced Bob and me as friends from America. She talked rapidly again and Elizabeth translated for us. "Pirip says that she's very thankful that you have come to visit her several times, and thankful for your small contributions for the women's association."

"Small? C'mon Pirip," I thought irritably, but her next words disarmed me.

"She says that her own mother and father died when she was young and she thinks of you and Bob as her mother and father." I cradled Pirip's shoulder and asked if I could speak. She nodded.

"I've known Pirip since 1983 when she was dreaming of a center for women and here we are, sitting in one today. I'm very proud of what she's done." Pirip's face glowed. I explained that I was writing a book about Papua New Guinea, and I was grateful to Pirip and her family and friends for helping me understand their country. Because of that, I wanted to make a donation to Pirip, as the president, for the work of the association—and I hoped they would consider using it for literacy training.

As Elizabeth translated my words, some of the women looked approving and several smiled.

"I would like very much to learn to read and write," said one young woman, and another identified herself as an English teacher in the school, and said she would be glad to help. "Are there women's groups in America, and what do they work for?" asked a third.

"Yes indeed," I said "Some women are beaten or deserted, just as they are here. Some are paid less than men for doing the same work, and there are still too few in our government. Women's groups work to change those things, and they are making good progress. I hope you will too." Then I urged them, as they worked for change in their lives, to keep thinking also about traditions that they want to preserve. There was more to be said, but the family was eager to move on.

"Now we're going to show you where mama lived in her childhood," Mike told us after Pirip intoned a closing prayer. With Paul's good-natured consent, we piled into the van, jockeying for space—Bob in front with Mike and Paul, Kuru, John, Gertrude, Elizabeth, Pirip, me, and several other women all in the back. Amidst laughter and chatter we turned south toward the Kumpor mountains, jouncing along a rough dirt road until we came to a roadside market.

"Stop, driver," Elizabeth commanded, and Paul did. We disentangled our limbs from each other and climbed out of the van. "This is my trade store," Elizabeth said proudly. "My daughter is the shopkeeper," and she led us into a small clean store with stock neatly stacked on the shelves behind the counter. There were tinned mackerel, cooking oil, sweet and savory biscuits, sugar, rice, candy, soap and laundry powder, and cigarettes. There was a cooler with soft drinks, and Bob treated us all to Coke, Sprite, or Fanta while I wondered about the effect of the sweet biscuits, candy, and soda on Pirip's splendid teeth.

Now the pilgrimage began in earnest as the road twisted, turned, dipped, and climbed steeply into precipitous mountains. As we drove alongside an agitated stream with smooth stones near its banks, Pirip turned to me.

"When I live up at the mission, they send me down here to fill my *bilum* with stones so they can make their building."

"So far down and back up again—hard work!" I sympathized.

"Very hard work," Pirip agreed. "But we love the missionaries so we think it's good work—we should do it voluntary."

"What did they do with the rocks?" Bob asked.

"Build houses and roads," she answered.

We climbed again, and when we came to a bridge high above white-water rapids and glimpsed a distant group of Western-style buildings, Bob twisted around and said to me, "We've been here before, you know. This is where Benjamin drove us in 1983 when we went up to see his parents' place. He told us there was a mission up there."

"That's so," Mike said. "That's the Swiss Evangelical Mission."

"These mountains look like the Swiss alps," I told him. "How did the missionary ever find them?"

"The missionary wanted to know where to do his work," Mike answered. "So he looked at a map of the world and a light was shining down on PNG. He put his finger there."

We twisted and climbed some more, and then Paul parked on the mission road. Now our legs did the climbing, up a steep, rocky lane to a sluice diverting a mountain stream toward a waterwheel. "To power the generator," Mike said as we walked across close-cropped lawns toward a stone church with a high peaked roof. Nearby, there was a grave of a woman missionary; 1926–1991 was incised in the headstone.

"She was like my mother," Pirip said, looking at it somberly

"Was that the girl who came to marry the missionary?" Bob asked.

"No, this one came as missionary from Switzerland. She stay at the mission; she did not marry," Pirip said sadly and spoke to Mike.

"Mum remembers, she was at a convention in Moresby when the lady died. Mum didn't attend the convention, she came up to attend the funeral."

"When did your real mother die?" I asked Pirip.

"Before I married; my father too." Leading Bob, Mike, and me to a rocky outcropping, she pointed still higher into the mountains. "Up there is Kamang where I was born."

"Could we go there?" I asked.

"Too far," said Mike. "The road is bad." Pirip and he began talking rapidly in pidgin, and Mike translated his mother's reminiscences.

At Christmas, when she did her grade three, there was a special ceremony at Kamang. It included young boys and girls, old people, middle-aged people, and they all enjoyed the ceremony. It was the ceremony of pig killing, thanking the gods because the people had many pigs. And it was a time to get together, Mike explained.

"Did it go on for many days or many weeks?" I asked.

"Six months," said Pirip. "Big celebration." She talked on to Mike, her glance darting between him and me.

"Mum says this was a holiday for all the people, for all their hard work. They come from far away. Now they stopped this custom—I don't know this custom, I just heard stories," Mike said uncertainly. "Mum says she was in school when this ceremony occurred and it interested her parents, her brothers, and all her relatives, so they sent a message for her to leave school and enjoy herself in the ceremony. Her brothers wanted strongly to take her out of school."

"I was interested in going to this ceremony," Pirip broke in, "but the missionaries, they go and look and come back and say, 'This is not good, you cannot go back and see this,' so I felt ashamed, but I said, 'I must go enjoy it myself,' so I came out of the mission."

"Maybe you felt two different ways," I said. "You wanted to go because it was a happy time but you also felt ashamed because the missionaries said it was wrong. That's hard—tradition pulling against the new way."

"Mm, hmm," Pirip and Mike chorused together, nodding. "Mum says, the missionaries came to her place several times and asked her to go back to school but her parents refused them. They said she must enjoy her young life, singing and dancing in the pig-killing celebration. Many other students left school too, because school was newly brought to their place and people didn't know what school meant to their life."

"I know there was a Kuma tradition to have ceremonies that helped turn a boy into a man. Was that part of the pig feast?" I asked. Pirip and Mike conferred solemnly for several minutes.

"I don't think it was part," said Pirip. "This was time for young men to look at young girls and decide whether they should get married." Her parents painted her face and decorated her with feathers and fur. "I was young, pretty, bright, and this was the great time to attract young men—I was requested by fifteen young men." Pirip's face was aglow, her eyes glistening like obsidian—a Melanesian Cinderella remembering the ball.

"Fifteen young men! Do you know your age when you left school?"

"Maybe eleven years old and I stayed with my parents at home for another five years and I was sixteen years old. Many people recognized that I was the most prettiest girl in the zone. Many young men, their parents come and ask my parents if they can marry me. Some parents of the young men kills pigs and brought them to my home and asked my parents if I could marry their sons. Sometimes I run away because of my parents' choice."

"You ran away?" I repeated. Pirip had been standing still, looking up into the alps as though she could see the scenes she described. She nodded.

"Some of the men who were interested to marry me, they were

middle-aged men, some were old men, they saw I was beautiful. They brought big pigs up and asked me to marry but I saw they were old men so I run away."

"Your parents didn't force you to come back?"

"I would go up to the mountains, to places where I look after pigs. It was very far away from where they live so they couldn't get me. I went up there and hided."

"Pirip, was Kuru one of the young men who wanted to marry you? Did you want to marry him?" Pirip nodded, strangely grim. Then she took a heedless step on the rocks, flinched, and reached toward one knee.

The memory flow interrupted, we moved slowly back toward the mission buildings. Straight-legged and bending from her hips, Pirip demonstrated how letters and numbers had been taught, incised with sharp stones on the earth or on lengths of split bamboo. Then she showed us the school building, with dormitories for boarders, and two rest houses. The memory of the one with seven sides gave her the idea for her *haus win,* she told me.

For some reason, Mike had suggested that Paul drive the van down a few loops in the road, and he went farther than expected. Both Pirip and Elizabeth were limping as we skidded down the steep roadway, both with painful knees.

"You're very fit," Elizabeth said to me.

"Bob and I walk a lot—our doctors say that is healthy, but my knees hurt sometimes too, and I brought Pirip some medicine I use." I had brought a bottle of Advil and later, in Mike's presence, I gave Pirip careful instructions about how to use it safely.

"We'll take you to visit the women's projects tomorrow," Elizabeth proposed when it was time for us to leave. "Pirip and I advise them, we help them with any problems and see if the money is being used well."

"You mean the projects they've started with their loans from the New Zealand grant?" I asked, and the women nodded.

"We'd like to see them," I said, and with promises that we would meet again tomorrow, we drove away, too worn out for conversation.

"You look tired," I told Pirip the next morning. Her eyes were inflamed and her hair stood up in stiff, matted tufts. "No, not tired," she said with a weary smile.

"She walked a long distance to a prayer meeting last night," Elizabeth explained. "She didn't get much sleep."

We piled into the van and set off for the projects. Where the road to Pirip's compound intersected with the highway, a new building stood out, the siding woven in diamond-shaped patterns.

"Stop, driver," Pirip said in a commanding tone, and we dismounted. This was Pirip's trade store, built with her loan from the New Zealand grant. She unlocked the door and took us into a clean room with a counter and shelves. But they were bare.

"I have to apply for another loan to buy stock," she said, and I felt a surge of sympathy, remembering Elizabeth's well-stocked store. But we congratulated Pirip on her excellent location. "I plan to continue the fence on down here," she said. More customers from the highway might also bring more risk of *rascols,* I supposed.

We went on to inspect a dozen projects close to the highway. At each stop, Pirip explained who Bob and I were, and we were met with smiles and handshakes. The older men, keening like Kuru's mother, all held my hand a surprisingly long time—Bob's too. After releasing my hand, each man flicked his own in the air as though shaking off water. I had asked Maggie about that the evening before, since a man near the lodge had done it.

"It is a way they communicate 'I hold you in high regard,'" she explained.

The projects included several trade stores and an "Automotive Clinic" with an elaborate sign painted by Pirip's son-in-law, Chris. The mechanic was a man, said Elizabeth as we walked through. "The women get the loans, but they are really family projects." Here the women's operation was a take-out shop. From behind a glassed-in case, a young woman was selling fried sausage, curlicues of fried dough, and *kaukau* glistening with grease and she spoke to Pirip.

"She asks if you would like one *kaukau*," Pirip told me. I declined with thanks—my chin held the memory of oozing grease.

"We'll show you an agricultural project," Pirip said, and we drove north down a long lane to a large cultivated field.

"They are growing white potatoes from seed," Elizabeth explained.

"To eat instead of *kaukau?*" I asked in dismay.

"No—to supply buyers in Moresby; the hotels want white potatoes for chips. The local people still eat *kaukau*. But there are problems here; the women are not cooperating, so they need to hire some workers." Elizabeth talked to the family in a nearby house, and then we drove back to the highway where we briefly visited two roadside displays of secondhand clothing, a piggery, and a chicken project where Pirip chose two live chickens and stuffed them into a sack.

"After two long days I think we need some meat tonight," she said. Two long days indeed; kaleidoscopic images and unanswered questions—more were to come.

As the afternoon waned, we gathered again in Pirip's house. Kuru sat slightly apart, near the kerosene stove, and Pirip directed him to heat water in the kettle and prepare coffee.

"There are a lot of different projects," I remarked.

"We only visited the ones that are closer today," Elizabeth said.

"How do you get to them—on the PMV?"

"Sometimes, but we usually use my vehicle," Elizabeth said. "We try to visit each one every week," she added, and Pirip sighed.

"I go every day. I have no time to be with my family any more."

"It's often like that in our country too," I said. "Let me tell you how it is with our children." I described the working lives of our daughter and son and their spouses—successful in their respective professions, but working up to ten hours a day and sometimes longer. "They can't choose whether to work or not to work, and they can't take time to travel to places like PNG. For Bob and me, it's different, especially now that we're over seventy and not working so much." Pirip and Elizabeth both frowned and their mouths gaped in surprise.

"You still go to work every day?"

"Oh yes," I said. "If we didn't work we wouldn't have enough money to travel to PNG or make contributions to your Women's Center." Pirip looked very solemn; after a troubled silence, she spoke.

"The law has changed. Now it's permitted for foreigners to join with nationals in business. Maybe when you're too old to travel here, we can give your son and daughter some land and they can come and start a business with us. Then the two families will stay together."

"We would like to stay joined with all of you," I said. By now, these warm people felt like extended family.

Gertrude had come in while we were talking, but John's wife did not. Each time we saw her today, she was sitting alone in the doorway of her house.

"What about John's wife, has her bride-price been exchanged yet—or is bride-price still your custom?" I asked the women.

"Yes, it's still well established," Elizabeth declared, explaining that the negotiations for John's wife's bride-price were not yet finished. "It's the custom for a wife to stay with her husband's family for five or more months while they negotiate and gather the bride-price. The amount is decided according to the value of the bride—her health, her age, and her educational level. One week ago we held a marriage feast for my own well-educated daughter," she said with a touch of hauteur. It had taken a long time to negotiate the price with the husband's parents. "We settled for seventy-five pigs, fifteen emus, and twelve thousand kina."

"Emus?" I hadn't heard them mentioned as a valuable before.

"Yes. Did you see the one outside?" Bob and I nodded. "We gave that one to Pirip and Kuru," Elizabeth told us proudly. "The custom is for the bride's parents to then give the husband's parents about half in each category," she went on, "so I and my husband gave thirty-seven pigs, seven emus, and six thousand kina. Then the bride's family gives a big feast. Then, after the birth of each child, there must be a pig-kill or else misfortune will come to the child."

Listening, I recalled my conversation about bride-price with Betty Kaman and Pirip in 1983. Had it actually been only

Westernized Betty and not Pirip who saw bride-price as a snare—and convinced me too?

"I was remembering our first meeting," I told Pirip. "I'm still not sure how you became interested in helping women change their lives." She was silent, frowning and looking down toward the floor, and then she began to talk in pidgin. Her voice was low and urgent, and her pidgin grew faster. I needed Elizabeth's help to understand.

"My father had three wives," Elizabeth translated. "I saw how he treated them." Pirip shook her head, as though trying to get free of the memory. "And I had seven brothers, no sisters. So I was the one who carried the water, I was the one who worked in the gardens. I was glad to leave my home and go to the missionary to have a different life.

"Then I met Kuru and I wanted to marry him. I came down to live with his people, but then he took another wife who was very jealous of me and she stabbed me many times." For the first time, Pirip stretched apart the plump folds of skin on her neck to show me an ugly scar hidden in a crease. Then she pulled up her sleeve to show me scars on her upper arm—I hadn't noticed them when she was bathing. "Then I knew I was back in the same life I had left as a child. I knew that I would work to make life better for women."

Kuru was sitting motionless, his face was inscrutable.

"What happened to the wife who stabbed you?" I asked.

"She stayed for five years and then she went away. She now lives in Australia."

"How much does it cost to go to America?" Elizabeth broke in. Maybe her unexpected question was prompted by the mention of Australia, but it interrupted the terse, bare-boned story and I was annoyed. Then Bob gave a rough estimate of round-trip group fare, and I could almost see wheels beginning to turn in Pirip's inventive mind.

"Maybe one day our group will go to America. Then *we* will go to visit *you*," she asserted with a smile. The thought buoyed our departure.

But today, for the very first time, Kuru didn't come to say good-bye.

◈ ◈ ◈

"Then I knew I was back in the same life I had left as a child." The tragedy of Pirip's words sank in slowly after we started back home. I often hear tales like that from clients in therapy—inadvertently recreating harmful experiences or relationships from the past, replaying old tapes. I had done that too.

My clients come to my office once a week, maybe twice, so that their stories can be explored in endurable increments. Trust builds slowly in my office. For many reasons, it had built more slowly in my dark-skinned sister across the world, and I felt impelled to go back. Partly to make sense of her story for myself, partly to let her know that her private life was as important as the public one. And maybe to finish what I hadn't finished with my blue-eyed, fair-skinned sister many years before.

So the frustrating exchange of letters began again.

◈ ◈ ◈

14 July 1996

Dear Audrey McCollum,
Hello and thank you very much for the letter that we received on the 9th of July. I, Mike, am very sorry for not replying your two previous letters. I was in prison for three months . . . I came home and Mum told me that you wrote two letters to her but she didn't trust anybody to write the reply letter, so she was waiting for me. Mum told that the letters were lost so we looked for the letters but couldn't find them.

Later I decided to write a new letter to you but from that moment my sister Ruth Selve was very sick so they send a message to us to visit her in Madang hospital. Me and Mum went and stayed with her for a month. After our staying in Madang we came home and Mum went to Manus for a workshop with the women's executives from all over the country. She stayed in

Manus for two weeks and she came home, and now she is still busy with the women executives to carry out the women's network programs.

Mum is very concern that you and her can stay together to complete the history book, so Mum is requesting you to write two letters. The first letter to the Governor of Western Highlands Province, and in your letter you can tell the Governor Mr. Pais Kengti about Pirip and yourself and ask him if he could arrange two tickets for us to fly down to America to stay with you and complete the history book. And the second letter to the Tribal Topps Inn at Mt. Hagen and ask Mr. Peter Van Fleet to donate some money to help Mum and me so that we will fly down and stay with you.

We will also write two letters to them and ask them to help because both of them know Mum personally. She works with the Government for twenty-five years and Mum is saying that if we write these letters to them, she is definitely sure that they will help us in arranging our tickets and money and we will stay together and finish our book in a short time. . . .

Finally I am going to write a new profile about Mum's history and everything that you have asked in your letter. From here I will pen off and may the Lord bless your family in your doing.

Your faithfully,
Mike Nombri
Pirip Til Kuru

When I showed this to Bob, we stared at each other, wondering what to do. Neither Mike nor Pirip had a way to envision the distance and expense involved. Or the fact that both would reel with culture shock. And worst of all, unfulfillable longings might be set in motion.

"I think visas would be a problem anyway," Bob said. "For Pirip, it may take a long time. For Mike, in trouble with the law, it's doubtful he'd get one this year." Phone calls to the PNG Embassy and the US State Department confirmed his suspicions.

So I wrote back, once again feeling like the voice of dreary reality, once again shattering her dreams. But I did agree that we needed more talk, and the Haus Poroman seemed the best place. We arranged that Pirip and Mike would stay there as our guests.

Chapter Sixteen

THE HEART OF THE STORY

"Did you see that, Bob?"
"See what?"

"An iridescent flash—in that tangle of trees right outside our cabin. So intense it didn't seem real."

"Maybe it wasn't," Bob teased, but he wheeled around with the binoculars raised. "It just landed, look up!" A bird was preening on a high branch, afternoon sunbeams rippling across his emerald, turquoise, and sapphire breastplate.

"Hallelujah, that's the superb bird of paradise our guide was talking about last year," I rejoiced. "How ironic; the first bird of paradise we saw in New Guinea—remember, at Baiyer River? I wonder if he'll be the last."

"Why d'you think . . . ?" Bob started to ask, but just then we heard a truck grinding up the hill, and we hurried toward the entrance into Haus Poroman—we'd been waiting for Pirip all day. As it happened, she had started out from Minj on the PMV, gone back to get Mike, and then set out again. At long last they were here, and Pirip's embrace was as strong, warm, and tearful as ever.

Her arms and cheeks looked plumper this year, and her *meri* blouse was fuller, while Mike had changed from youth into man. His mien appeared grim—the nuances of his expression obscured by a beard and dark sunglasses—and his hair stood up in short, stiff tufts. Hardened by recent happenings? Perhaps, but his greeting was friendly.

After surveying the bungalow assigned to them—Pirip's darting glance seemed to absorb all the details—they joined us in ours for the first of several long conversations. Each time we talked, another layer of Pirip's story was disclosed.

Mike had brought a summary of the events of his mother's life, handwritten on lined paper. That had been a laborious task, I judged; when I asked him about a name he had put down, he brought his head within inches of the paper. And when he took off his sunglasses in the bungalow's dim light, he revealed a damaged left eye.

"You've hurt your eye!" I blurted out—the whole socket appeared sunken and the lid was partly closed in a painful looking squint. He didn't answer. He slipped the glasses back on as though he were ashamed and never explained the injury.

"Your history will help a lot, Mike, and I'll read it carefully later," I told him. "But I hope Pirip will talk with me about her memories too." She nodded, so we gathered around the wooden table near the open door. Pirip accepted the straight-backed chair at our insistence; Bob and Mike teetered on up-ended logs, and I sat on the edge of the bed.

"When we were talking up at the mission last year," I reminded Pirip, "you told us that fifteen young men wanted to marry you when you were a girl." Pirip murmured and shook her head, as she always did when I recalled our shared past—as though she were either amazed at my memory or surprised that she mattered that much to me. "You said, 'One of them was my husband.' That was Kuru, right? You wanted to marry him?"

"Yes, he was handsome and I loved him and I married him," she said, but her voice sounded joyless.

"Was there a bride-price?" I asked. Pirip answered in rapid pidgin and Mike translated. That would happen many times during this visit; Pirip would follow Mike's answers closely and, occasionally, correct them, but she used less English than the year before. Maybe the emotions being stirred up interfered with her recall of English words.

"Mum says it was in the olden days, so my father brought pigs and feathers and gave it to her family," Mike told me. "He walked with the pigs all the way from Minj; it was maybe twenty kilometers and there were no roads." Kuru's desire for Pirip must have been intense, I thought, recalling our own off-road hikes through Tari Basin and the Schrader mountains. We followed steep, narrow clay tracks that became grease-slippery after a rain. And there were sometimes leeches.

"Pirip," I said, reining in those memories, "you told us last year that you're gathering bride-price for your son, John, so maybe you think bride-price is still a good custom."

"Yes, yes," said Mike, "I think this is a good custom because the traditional way of doing things is all gone; this is the only tradition that still remains."

"You think that, Mike, but does Pirip think that too?"

"Mum says she thinks it's bad, wastes a lot of money and pigs, but this is our custom, it is passed on so we have to do this. We give bride-price to get a big name and get known to other people. If we don't give bride-price they will say, 'You don't have anything.'"

"You mean other people usually know how big the bride-price is?" Bob asked.

"Yes, everybody knows. Mum says, at first she had no bride-price when she got married to my father. Later he gave pigs and feathers, then later when we got born he gave 2,400 kina to her family—that was money."

"Did you have a Christian ceremony or a traditional one, Pirip?"

"Traditional wedding, in Minj," Pirip answered directly and spoke on.

"When Mum got married her face was painted and she was dressed in furs and decorated with feathers," Mike translated. "She was carried around by Kuru's father's brothers' sons, and then this was the end of the ceremony."

"You must have been beautiful, Pirip," I said, and now her smile brought radiance to her face and exposed both rows of her splendid teeth. "When John got married, did your family carry the girl the same way?"

"It will be done," Mike answered. "Mum's saying, 'I just thought of asking you to witness the bride-price ceremony. I'll write to you guys.'"

"So you feel different ways," I ventured. "Bride-price is a waste of pigs but it's also a tradition that gives pleasure. Is that right?"

"That is right " Pirip murmured wearily, and then she stifled a yawn.

"Well, you've had a long and tiring day," I said. "Let's stop telling stories now. We'll meet in the big *haus* for the evening meal at seven, and tomorrow, after we've all had a good sleep, we can talk some more."

◈ ◈ ◈

The mists were thick the next morning, swirling out of the cloud forest that surrounded the lodge, muffling birdsong and even human voices. Some of the vapors blew into our cabin, making it seem like a stage set in which some sinister drama would be played out.

"Pirip," I said when we'd gathered there again after breakfast, "either you or Elizabeth told me last year that your father didn't treat his wives so well. Did you mean that he beat them?" Pirip frowned and shook her head.

"The father—never," she answered.

"Then I didn't understand," I said. "But yesterday, Mike, you said there's more to the story that you didn't have time to write about—you mentioned family trouble." Now Pirip nodded, and I shivered in the chilly dampness. Leaning heavily on her forearms, gazing down at the table top, Pirip spoke in a low, urgent voice as Mike translated.

"Mum says, when she got married she thought that it was good to marry Kuru, and then later she realized there were many troubles in her life. When she got married to my father, he stayed only one month with my mother, and then he went out and brought five other ladies. After he married Mum he married five others."

"All at once?" Bob sounded astonished.

"At first, two came together, then the other three came—one came later, one came later, one came later. He never stayed with Mum; he went around looking at ladies and never thought of Mum."

"Maggie Wilson told me some women are happy to have another wife to share the work. Were you ever happy to have another wife in the family?" I asked. Pirip shook her head, looking grim, and spoke very fast.

"Mum says no, not happy. But she followed the way she was brought up at the mission, so she didn't get angry at the ladies who came to marry Kuru." Then things got worse, Mike explained. Kuru gave her house to another wife. He came to the house where Pirip slept, the *haus bilong slip* he had built for her, and told her to get out of his house.

"What did you do, Pirip?" I asked.

"Mum went out," said Mike. "She followed the Christian way, never to get angry and never talk bad."

"You never showed anger but did you feel angry inside?" Pirip met my gaze and nodded.

"Yes, feel anger but never show it out," she said in a low, intense voice.

"So did Kuru build a new house for you?"

"Never," she said. "I stay with Kuru's father."

"And when Kuru brought the other four wives, did he build new houses for any of them?" I asked.

"No. Four ladies that he brought were given to other relatives but he gave Mum's house to the fifth lady, so Mum had to go with my father's father," Mike explained. I took a couple of slow, deep breaths, in a state akin to the one Pirip described—feeling anger inside but not feeling free to "show it out."

"Pirip, when your husband went off with other women after one month with you, did you think of going back to your family?" I asked after a pause. Pirip bowed her head. Her face was almost devoid of expression, but light from the doorway flickered across her lower lip as words rushed out of her mouth.

"She don't want to go back because people would say that she was a married lady who left her husband and they would not love her," said Mike.

"They would blame her?"

"Yes, they would think she was some kind of—at the young stage of life there were many young men she loved. They might say bad things that would hurt her feelings." I supposed that Pirip was referring to her teenage years, the time when Kuma girls had been encouraged to take the initiative in sexual encounters—the time of courting parties. Too, I recalled that a Kuma woman who left her husband was traditionally seen as a sexual predator, a "Wandering Woman" trying to attach herself to other men.

"You would have felt ashamed, Pirip?" I ventured.

"Ashamed, yes," Pirip affirmed; she nodded without looking up.

"Even though it was Kuru who made the trouble, you would have felt ashamed." That weighed heavily on me; I had heard similar disclosures from American women—all too often. "Was there another reason too? If you'd wanted to go away from Kuru, would it have been a problem because the bride-price would have to be paid back?" I asked. Betty Kaman had told me that in our first meeting with Pirip.

"Mum says, if she had gone back to her family, the bride-price should have been given back to my father, so she had to stay with him," said Mike.

"But would your family have been *able* to give it back?"

"Yes, they could have given back the bride-price to my father but Mum thought, if I go back to my family my name will have been spoiled—she didn't want to go back. She stayed with Dad," Mike explained.

Kuma tradition and Christian teaching seemed to have caught Pirip in an unyielding trap. I was silenced by a sense of hopelessness, and nobody else spoke either.

Then Bob broke the silence. "In the mission, did they teach you one husband, one wife?" and Pirip nodded again. "And what did they think about Kuru taking other wives? Did you tell the missionaries?"

"They hear it," she said. "They watch me, they look after me."

"Did you go back to the mission, Pirip?"

"Yes later, after Ruth was born," she told us, then said more to Mike.

"So my father got married to five other ladies," Mike repeated, as though to anchor us in this troubling tale. "The fifth lady, she got anger and she fought the other ladies. She took out a knife and thrust it in Mum." Pirip held out her arms and pointed to more scars than she had shown us last year; her eyes filled with tears. "When Mum got this beating, Father never came and talked to her," Mike went on, looking grim.

"Never came to help your mum?"

"No. But the missionaries saw this was no good, so they took her," Mike explained. "She stayed there one year, eight months."

"With Ruth?" asked Bob.

"Ruth and the other son."

"There was another son?"

"Yes, he was about two years old and then died."

"Before Ruth or after Ruth?" Bob's search for chronology was insistent, maybe to dilute the horror of what we were hearing. I felt shattered. Betrayed by Kuru—by that grizzled man who had greeted me with hugs and tears, who had seemed gentle and kind and dedicated to helping his wife in her work for women.

"It was after Ruth," said Mike. "When my father did this to Mum, Mum prayed and asked the Lord to help her. She knew that the Lord was the only way."

"Was that before the missionaries came to take her?" asked Bob.

"That was before." This came from Pirip.

"Then the missionaries came to take you?"

"Later. Mum said she was praying until the Lord sent the missionaries to take her away."

"An answer to her prayer," Bob suggested gently, and Pirip agreed.

"Let's stop for a few minutes," I proposed, exhausted by the effort to untangle this harrowing tale. "Why don't you go down to the lounge, ask for a cup of coffee or tea and have a rest?" Our guests went off and Bob and I walked around the gardens. The sun had blazed through the mists by now, and we drew in the pure air and the rising birdsong, trying to counteract this saga of human ugliness. Yet dew drops clinging to the flowers looked to me like tears this morning.

Mike and Pirip were back sooner than we expected—another layer of her story was pressing to be told. So we reassembled inside.

"Pirip, can you tell us what happened after Ruth was born?" I asked quietly, wondering whether this was an ordeal for her or a relief.

Kuru took Ruth away from Pirip and gave her to the fifth lady to look after, Mike explained, adding, "So then Mum and Dad got another baby. Later the missionaries heard this story, so they came and took Ruth away from that lady; then they took Mum and this baby away from my father's place and took them to the mission station."

"How long had the fifth wife looked after Ruth?" Bob wondered, still needing a coherent time frame.

"For three months, maybe two months, and then the missionaries came and said 'This is not your daughter' and took Ruth away." When Pirip went to the missionaries, they gave her a house and a block of coffee trees to look after, Mike recounted. When they sold the coffee, they shared the money with Pirip. "The house was for the house girl, but one room was given to Mum. She was there with Ruth and the baby. The missionaries told Mum they will get a summons to divorce my father and then they will send her to Bible school down at the coast, at Lae, but she said no. She didn't want to go. Her Christian life and her Christian faith was very strong. She thought that her husband was waiting for her."

I felt a surge of exasperation. Her mentors would have sanctioned divorce, but she couldn't let go of that destructive marriage. Was the threat of shame so strong? The threatened loss of status as wife? A spasm of tension was gripping my back—it gathers there when I hear an unbearable story and have to contain my responses. "Then did you leave the mission and go back to Kuru?" I asked, but there was still another layer of the story.

"At first," Mike reiterated patiently, "when father married the fifth wife, that lady came and fight Mum." Pirip spoke rapidly again, her face somber, her voice intense. Maybe her emotions were as tightly controlled as mine—or more so. "Mum says Kuru tied Mum with barbed wire and allowed this wife to cut her with a knife, and she cut the baby too. Mum took him to hospital and he stayed for two months and later the small boy died."

"Died from the cutting?" I asked and Pirip nodded. "So he died after Pirip left the missionaries?" Even knowing that traumatic memories swirl in a timeless vortex, I, too, was reaching for the sequence of the story, maybe to deflect my mind from the ghastly image of a bloodied infant.

"Before she left," Mike said, still patient. "Mum was very worried and sad. The missionaries sent a message to my father that the baby was dead and asked, 'Are you coming to take him to bury him at your place or will we bury him in the station?' The missionaries gave a coffin to Mum to bury the child. The missionaries told my father, 'You will be judged later by the Lord.'"

"Do you think Kuru was sorry?" I asked, realizing that I'd probably never know whether the infant had died in the hospital or later at the mission—and that it really didn't matter. What mattered was that Pirip's infant son had been slaughtered and her husband helped that happen.

"I don't know if he was sad for his son," said Mike. "He brought the dead body back and he went around with his other wife."

"Did he have other children by the other wives?" Bob wondered.

"No other children. The fifth lady was tough and she was trying to fight them all the time so the other wives went away. The fifth was the only one left."

"Maybe she was fighting because she was jealous," I ventured, and Pirip agreed. It was Kuru's visits to the other wives that would spark the fights.

"But why did you decide to go back and live with him again?" I kept my voice measured with an effort. Pirip let out an explosive laugh—it sounded bitter—and spoke rapidly again.

"Mum says, 'I was thinking I was the first wife and it was not good that I go out. I should follow my Christian faith and go back.'"

"Did Kuru accept her?" Bob asked Mike.

"The missionaries got a summons and gave it to my father. So this was Mum's only chance to get a summons to district court. He was sent to court."

"So the summons helped get her back—he was under court order to take her back," Bob clarified, and both Pirip and Mike nodded.

"Then you came back to Kuru and wife number five was still there," I said to Pirip. She nodded and talked on urgently.

"This lady and Mum, they were fighting," said Mike. "This lady was trying to kill Mum's next baby too—that was Gertrude. Mum covered Gertrude's head with her hand and this lady got a knife into Mum's hand. So they got the missionary, who sent Mum to Chimbu to teach pidgin. The fifth wife was sent to prison for six months."

"Sent to prison because she cut your mother?"

"Yes. Later, when she came out of prison she was married to this other man and then divorced him, then she was married to a white man from Australia. Now they are in PNG; they are in business in Minj, Madang, Goroka, Australia."

"Pirip, when she cut you, did you think she was going to kill you?"

"Mum says yes, she thought of killing. When Mum was holding Gertrude, the lady came forward and she was going to thrust the knife into Gertrude, so Mum held her hand over Gertrude to prevent the knife."

"She wanted to kill your babies—she had no babies, so she was jealous?" Pirip nodded; her eyes had reddened and mine were prickling with unshed tears.

"Mike, what feelings did you have when you heard this story?" I asked. He had kept his voice neutral as he interpreted the grisly tale, and now he just shook his head and answered indirectly.

"My brother, John, he wanted to kill my father when he heard this story. We had to hold him back." Then Mike explained that he, himself, had heard things today he'd never heard before. He looked grim, and we sat in silence. Eight shoulders seemed to sag.

"Pirip, was it because of this fifth wife that you decided you wanted to work for women?" I asked after a few moments, standing to stretch my knotted back.

"Mum says she faced a lot of problems since she got married, and she thought all the women around the country also faced this same kind of problem, and the Bible says that man and woman are equal. So she thought it is not good for man to beat his wife or marry another woman—and then she thought of asking government to set up a committee or woman's group. So Mum started this women's group and she was selected as president."

"What year was that?" Bob asked.

"1974," said Mike tentatively.

"1976," Pirip corrected him, although Mike's date agreed with his written "history."

"You had how many children then, Pirip?" inquired Bob.

"It was Mike and John, Ruth and Gertrude at this time," she said.

"Did I understand that you read in the Bible that man and woman are equal—is that what you said?" I asked Pirip and she agreed. She read in the Bible that God made Adam and God made Eve, so man and woman are equal, she explained.

"And women told you they were having the same sorts of problems?" I asked and Pirip nodded again. She explained that she had taught a pidgin class and women came to her and asked her advice about how to face their troubles with their husbands. She told them that they must listen to what the Bible says and stay with their husbands. They must carry the troubles they were facing; when their husbands fought them, they musn't fight back but just go away.

"Mum is saying that every time she went and slept with other ladies she came back to the house; she washed my father's clothes and carried water for washing. She told the other ladies, you will do this for your husband," Mike added.

"Was this back in Minj?" Bob asked and Pirip agreed. Her brothers had come down to build her a new house by then.

"It was because she was the only girl and they loved her, that's why they came down to help her," Mike said. "She's the only sister they have."

"Whose land did they build on?" asked Bob.

"In those times there were not many people here, so she put some money aside, 1,000 kina, from what the mission gave her. She bought some wire and fenced it in."

"Then it was your land, not Kuru's?" said Bob, sounding surprised.

"Yes, my land," said Pirip.

"Did you have to buy the land?"

"No, just claim it," she explained, and we sat quietly for a minute.

"Do you think Kuru is sorry those things happened?" I asked, struggling to reconcile the image of Kuru in this ugly tale with my memories of him.

"When we were born, he realized we were a good family and he loved us," said Mike. "He never said to Mum that he did bad things to her, but he told other people. One day he bought a double mattress. He told Mum, 'Here is a present for you.' That's the only thing he has done to help her.

"Now everyone sees that Mum is working strongly for women. She looked after us, she paid our school fees—all done by Mum. And Mum is always going to contribute money for bride-price or other ceremonies.

"My father, he feels sorry for himself. He plants a lot of coffee, he looks after bananas—it is on Mum's land. He gets some money when he sells the coffee and bananas and then he usually helps us in small ways—clothes, goods—he tries to help us."

"Does he stay with you?"

"In daytime, yes. He sleeps in the trade store."

"He used to go to the men's house; when did he stop going there?"

"For a long time. There are no more men's houses—well, there are two or three. Sometimes we go there and hang around. Sometimes Dad sleeps with John and his wife and the old woman—my father's mother." In spite of Kuru's cruelty, I felt a heavy pity stirring. Was it guilt that spurred him to support Pirip in her work for women? Or was that support his effort to find a respected place in a rapidly changing world? I'd probably never know.

"Ruth is where?" Bob's question interrupted my musings.

"Ruth and Chris are living in Minj, doing God's work. Gertrude stays at home, she has her own little house. She's a single lady and she has three pigs, or maybe two."

"Your trade store, Pirip, have you been able to get it operating yet?" I asked her and she shook her head. The carpenter was her brother; he was working at a job and hadn't had time to finish building the store.

"And what about your plans for the center?"

"Mum wrote letters to departments and to people trying to find money to build three or four of this kind of house," Mike said, gesturing toward the woven pandanus walls of our bungalow. They had posted a notice at the Gateway Hotel by the airport in Port Moresby, and two groups came to stay in the *haus win,* but one group left because of the lack of facilities. "We're hoping to get electricity and have light and a pump for water—later, maybe television. Wiring is ready in one house but we don't have posts to bring light from town."

"Chris is an electrician, isn't he? Can he help you?" I asked.

"Yes, but he's busy, he's making another store at the junction so we don't trust him to help us."

"You've had a lot of difficulties to overcome," I said. "But you should be very proud of what you've done in your life—do you feel proud, Pirip?"

"Yes," she answered, lifting her face. Light reflected off her forehead and the plump mounds over her cheekbones. She talked on.

"Mum says, 'I'm happy because I get a lot from the outside world and also I am really glad and happy that I have you as my parents.' That's what Mum always says: 'I love you and I always thought that you were my real parents. I have been in a lot of trouble and have carried this until now, and now I see that a lot of people come and help me like you guys, and some people have been here all this time. I see God in women's work, and God is always with me and that is why I'm never worried about anything. In the first place when Kuru did this, when I first had trouble, I thought that if I divorced him all those bad things would happen to me. I just didn't know. But I was in a Christian life and I can see that He was near.'"

"Even when you were a young girl you were very strong," I reminded her, and Pirip and Mike hummed their agreement together. "You've always been a *strongpela meri*." Pirip laughed, her full lips opening in a wide curve, her face looking happy. "Now many people know about your work—that's very fine. I imagine you're proud of your mum, Mike."

"I be proud of my mum."

"Bob and I are proud of you too, Pirip," I added and she spoke again.

"Mum says people ask, 'Why does this white woman and man come to see you so many times? Why do they contribute to the center?' They say, 'Maybe they are your own father and mother come back from the dead.'"

I nodded, recalling the Jesus pictured in Pirip's house—a man with translucently white skin who was resurrected from the dead. That depiction of Christian belief may have reinforced traditional beliefs about the return of the dead. Or traditional beliefs and Christianity may have easily converged.

Then Pirip looked directly at me, her eyes moist and lustrous.

"I wish," she said, "I wish that you really *are* my mother." She paused and her gaze darted toward Bob. "And I wish you really *are* my father."

Neither Bob nor I could speak.

EPILOGUE

We left Papua New Guinea two days later—honored by Pirip's trust, moved by her affection, and awed by the obstacles she had overcome.

Except for their adolescent years, during which Kuma girls joined together to enjoy courting parties and the lovemaking that followed, there was little tradition of female bonding among Pirip's people. A woman's prime loyalties were directed toward men: her brothers and other members of her clan-of-birth; later, her husband and his clansmen. Co-wives often lived at a distance from each other, too far apart for easy, everyday interaction. If they came from hostile clans, they were suspicious of one another. Even if they came from congenial clans, they were prone to jealousy—Pirip's story was a grim testimonial to that.

Her letters had made it clear that some women worked with her in the association briefly, and then left to pursue their own interests. There seemed to be little loyalty to a common cause. And, as another impediment, the more privileged women in the towns and cities weren't necessarily concerned with the needs of rural women.

But Pirip persisted. As she drew women into the South Wahgi Women's Association (of which I'm a proud member), theirs was not a separatist movement as some Western feminist movements have been. The snooker table that had puzzled and exasperated me was, I now realized, both reality and metaphor. As women accumulated cash, they were contributing to the collective needs of family or clan: compensation payments, bride-price, clothing, tinned fish. And as small loans were distributed to women, they were being invested in family projects. The aim was not independence *from* men but collaboration *with* men as respected partners—an aim most United States women would gladly embrace.

When Bob and I visited Minj in 1992 and found that Pirip was away, we talked with Chris and Ruth about changes in Wahgi Valley. I told Chris that I had seen people carrying plastic bags in the Mt. Hagen market. I told him we have learned that discarded plastic clutters the land; it doesn't rot and return to the earth. For that reason, many people in our region carry cloth bags or net bags. I take my Wahgi *bilum* to market. Chris' face pleated itself into a big grin and he said, "We want to be like you and you want to be like us!" There was some truth in that.

The frantic pursuit of cash, and the goods it can buy, has taken a toll on life in my country. Many people live in luxurious homes, wear elegant clothes, drink single malts, drive Mercedes convertibles, and exist in states of misery—anxious, depressed, deeply lonely. Being a fiscal superstar is not enough. Even people whose wants are more modest work long hours, and splits are widening between husbands and wives, parents and children.

Security and contentment bloom in a field of personal relationships. Those desirable states arise from responding to others and having them respond in turn. They arise from helping and being helped. They arise from having one's abilities appreciated and appreciating the abilities of others. They arise from liking and feeling liked, loving and feeling loved. These are all reciprocal experiences, and they require a social context—an affirming community of some sort. Yet the sense of community has been eroded in the United States.

But winds of change are sweeping through certain areas of the country; the Upper Valley, where I now happily live, is among them. Wise people here are looking back at the older traditions, especially the cohesion of agrarian life or of ethnic neighborhoods in our cities. They are searching out the gathering places—the farmers' markets, country stores, skating ponds, coffee houses—where people share news, trade jokes, and express concern for each other. They are designing forums through which people can be spurred to envision the communities in which they want to live, and then take cooperative action to transform their visions into realities.

My travels in Papua New Guinea have honed my interest in those efforts and, all around me, I see the very thing Pirip and I talked about in Minj. People are beginning to understand that the best kind of change keeps the best traditions alive. The best kind of change honors the old while it celebrates the new. I hope that Pirip will find ways to do those things too.

◈　◈　◈

She was often in my thoughts, but many months slid by before I understood why our last meeting had affected me so deeply. Then I knew this book would become a reality.

5 July 1998

My dear Pirip,

It has been a long time since we sat together in Haus Poroman, the "house of friends." I have thought about that day many times. Now I want to try and tell you how I felt when you said, "I wish you really *are* my mother."

It seems odd that you wish I were your mother, because I've often wished that my own mother had been like you—strong and brave and persistent, taking care of yourself, your children, and other women too when your husband had been cruel. My mother's husband (my father) was cruel—maybe not in a physical way, but he left her alone with her children again and again, and then he went to another woman. He was a strong man in his body but not in his mind; maybe Kuru was like that too. My mother was not strong either, not like you. She couldn't take care of herself or her children.

As to being like a mother to you, I'm not sure I have been a good one. When I first met you, I was in the midst of a big change in my life. I was happy to support you in your work for women. I thought it was important work, and it helped me feel useful.

Then I began to worry and have doubts. I could see how bringing people into modern ways—especially the cash economy—was causing many women to lose the influence and power they had in their traditional lives. Gabriel Waipek told us that in

1989 when we met in your fine *haus win*, and I heard the same thing later in the Tari Women's Center. I began urging you to think about the traditions that you do *not* want to lose.

But when you told me the story of your married life, I knew that you were right to want certain changes. As you have said, women must be able to make their own choices and take care of themselves, even without a man.

Maybe the interest and support of an American woman did give you some encouragement—I hope that has been true. But I know that I disappointed you many times because I couldn't do all the things that you wanted. Yet, even though I disappointed you, it seems that you could still want me as a mother. You must have understood that I cared about you and really tried to help.

I disappointed my own mother and my younger sister many times too, because I couldn't do what they wanted either. They are both dead and I'll never know whether they realized how much I cared about them. But your feelings toward me help me to see that I really did my best—for you and for them. Your feelings toward me help me to forgive myself for not being able to do more. Your feelings toward me tell me that I am a good person even if I often fail and make mistakes.

Thank you for that gift, my dear Pirip. This book is my gift to you.

With love from Bob and from me,
Audrey

Pirip's answer came soon, written once again by Mike. They were very surprised to receive my letter, he said, because there had been an accident at the time of our flight back to the United States. A plane had crashed, and they thought we must be on it. They had been very sad—but now they felt fine again.

Pirip was extremely busy, Mike continued, because there were three loan programs in operation. She and the family had succeeded in bringing electricity into the center, and Pirip was trying to find funds to bring water in too. Then she hoped to build a guest house.

Except for Kuru's mother, who died last year, the whole family was fine and living in the highlands, Mike wrote. Besides Pirip and Kuru, the family now included Ruth, Chris, and their children; Gertrude; John and his wife, Macky, with a small daughter also named Pirip; Mike and his new wife, Julie; and Stanley.

On reflection, I wondered how fine Kuru could really be. That exuberant man had greeted us joyfully in 1995. But then, after Pirip began telling the story of their marriage, he melted away. He failed to say good-bye when we left—as though he were ashamed. When we heard the full story during our next visit, I'd felt outraged at first, then deeply sad to learn of the dark side of his nature. I wondered how he felt about himself.

Over the years, Pirip's letters had mentioned ways in which Kuru was helping her: building traditional houses in her center; taking care of the children while she was busy with women's affairs. And he drove with her to meet us in Madang. True, Kuru had never told Pirip in words that he was sorry for his earlier cruelties. But maybe he was expressing remorse through his actions. Trying to make amends. Asking her to forgive him.

Some day I would broach that with her—she seemed like a forgiving woman. She was toward me; Mike conveyed that in his letter.

> Mama Pirip is saying: You are living far away from Papua New Guinea but you always write to me to check whether I am fine, and sometimes you fly to my country to visit me and that really makes me feel great about you. Whether you disappoint me or not I really love you in my heart and I always love you forever.

BIBLIOGRAPHY

Brown, Paula. 1978. *Highland Peoples of New Guinea.* Cambridge: Cambridge University Press.

Connolly, Bob and Robin Anderson. 1987. *First Contact. New Guinea's Highlanders Encounter the Outside World.* New York: Viking Penguin.

Errington, Frederick and Deborah Gewertz. 1987. *Cultural Alternatives and a Feminist Anthropology.* Cambridge: Cambridge University Press.

Frankel, Stephen. 1986. *The Huli Response to Illness.* Cambridge: Cambridge University Press.

Gewertz, Deborah and Frederick Errington. 1991. *Twisted Histories, Altered Contexts. Representing the Chambri in a World System.* Cambridge: Cambridge University Press.

Glasse, Robert M. 1965. *The Huli of the Southern Highlands.* In *Gods, Ghosts and Men in Melanesia,* edited by P. Lawrence and M.J. Meggitt, 27–49. Oxford: Oxford University Press.

Herdt, Gilbert, ed. 1982. *Rituals of Manhood. Male Initiation in Papua New Guinea.* Berkeley: University of California Press.

MacCormack, Carol P. and Marilyn Strathern, eds. 1980. *Nature, Culture and Gender.* Cambridge: Cambridge Univeristy Press.

McCollum, Audrey. 1990. *The Trauma of Moving. Psychological Issues for Women.* Newbury Park: Sage Publications.

McCollum, Audrey, Nadia Jensen, and Stuart Copans. 1996. *Smart Moves. Your Guide through the Emotional Maze of Relocation.* Lyme: Smith and Kraus, Inc.

O'Brien, Denise and Sharon W. Tiffany, eds. 1984. *Rethinking Women's Roles. Perspectives from the Pacific.* Berkeley: University of California Press.

Reay, Marie. 1959. *The Kuma. Freedom and Conformity in the New Guinea Highlands.* Melbourne: Melbourne University Press.

Schneebaum, Tobias. 1988. *Where the Spirits Dwell. An Odyssey in the Jungle of New Guinea*. New York: Grove Press.

Semana, Utula. 1988. *Papua New Guinea: Which Way?* Victoria: Arena Publications.

Strathern, Andrew J., ed. 1982. *Inequalities in New Guinea Highland Societies*. Cambridge: Cambridge University Press.

Strathern, Marilyn. 1972. *Women in Between. Female Roles in a Male World: Mt. Hagen, New Guinea*. London: Seminar Press.

Strathern, Marilyn, ed. 1987. *Dealing with Inequality. Analyzing Gender Relations in Melanesia and Beyond*. Cambridge: Cambridge University Press.

Turner, Ann. 1993. *Views from Interviews. The Changing Role of Women in Papua New Guinea*. Melbourne: Oxford University Press.

Waiko, John D. 1993. *A Short History of Papua New Guinea*. Melbourne: Oxford University Press.

GLOSSARY

Aibika — an edible leaf

As — buttocks

As gras — a bunch of long, narrow leaves worn to cover the buttocks

Bel — abdomen

Belihat — state of anger or lust

Big Man — clan or subclan leader who has achieved status through skill at oratory and negotiation, not by inheritance

Bilas — ceremonial dress or ornamentation of body

Bilum — net bag made by looping strings of fiber

Bisnis — trade, business, living

Cuscus — marsupial often called tree kangaroo

Erima — large, semi-hardwood tree

Garamut — a hardwook tree; drum made from a hollowed-out length of garamut

Gutpela — good, kind, tasty

Haus bilong slip — house for sleeping

Haus kai — house where food is sold

Haus liklik or *haus pispis* — toilet

Haus man — men's house

Haus tambaran — spirit house; center for sacred rituals

Haus win — rest house (from *kesim win,* to rest)

Ibagiyanda — a bachelor cult house

Kaikai — food

Kaukau — sweet potato

Kunai — sword grass

Kundu — hourglass-shaped drum with an aminal or reptile skin stretched taut over one end

Kwila — hardwood tree

Laplap — loincloth or length of cloth tied around the waist

Limbom — tall, slender hardwood palm

Masalai — demon or evil spirit inhabiting a special place

Meri — native woman

Mismaster bilong Jesus Christ — helicopter

Mumu — earth oven; a feast baked in an earth oven

Pandanus — plant with sword-shaped leaves arranged in a spiral

Payback — reciprocal gift, assistance, or revenge

Pigbel — dangerous intestinal infection, often a consequence of pig feasts

Pitpit — wild sugar cane; some forms are edible

Ples tok — language of the place

Rascols — those who engage in crime; usually idle young men

Sago palm — any of several tropical, old-world plants that yield sago

Sago — starchy foodstuff prepared from the soft interior of a sago palm

Singsing — ceremonial dancing and song

Strongpela — strong

Strongpela meri tru — really strong woman

Tambaran — spirit or ghost inhabiting a special place

Tambu — forbidden

Tanim — turn, twist, revolve

Tanket — plant whose colorful leaves are used in ceremonies and to cover the buttocks

Taro — tropical plant that yields an edible tuber

Ton — large hardwood tree

Tru — true, really

Wantok — people who speak the same language

INDEX

COMPILED BY STEVE CHUPACK

THE AUTHOR

Audrey McCollum was born and raised in New York City, where turmoil in her family sparked her drive to become a psychotherapist and writer. Educated at Vassar College and the Simmons College School of Social Work, she became a family therapist and research associate at the Yale University Child Study Center and Department of Pediatrics. During those years, she married and began rearing her daughter and son.

Her first book, *Coping with Prolonged Health Impairment in Your Child* (Little Brown and Co.) was described as "the best book in the field with the worst title!" Expanded and updated, it was later published as *The Chronically Ill Child: A Guide for Parents and Professionals* (Yale University Press).

A move to New Hampshire kindled her interest in personal transition. Her groundbreaking book, *The Trauma of Moving: Psychological Issues for Women* (Sage Publications) was followed by *Smart Moves: Your Guide Through the Emotional Maze of Relocation* (Smith and Kraus), co-authored by Nadia Jensen and Stuart Copans.

An avid traveler, drawn to the beauty and mystery of tropical coral reefs and rain forests, Ms. McCollum became fascinated by Papua New Guinea—a nation in the midst of tumultuous change. During repeated visits there, she and a rural activist, Pirip Kuru, developed the complex and ever-deepening friendship described in *Two Women, Two Worlds*.

Ms. McCollum practices psychotherapy, writes, skis, hikes, and lives happily with her husband in Etna, New Hampshire.